ave par Tardieu l'ain.

This drawing of a Shawnee Indian, printed in the early 1800's, was furnished by the Ohio State Historical Society.

A JOURNAL *of* TWO VISITS MADE TO SOME
NATIONS *of* INDIANS *on* THE WEST SIDE
of THE RIVER *OHIO*, IN THE YEARS
1772 *and* 1773.

The David Jones, *A Journal of Two Visits* . . . is No. J-208 in Wright Howes' U.S.-IANA. Three hundred copies were printed by Glen Adams with the first copies being bound in the early summer of the year of Our Lord, one-thousand-nine-hundred-seventy-three.

This is Copy number 3 0 .

A JOURNAL of TWO VISITS MADE TO SOME NATIONS of INDIANS on THE WEST SIDE of the RIVER OHIO, in the YEARS 1772 and 1773.

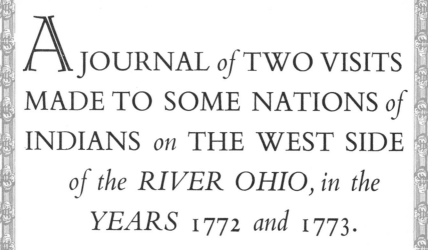

Rev. DAVID JONES

YE GALLEON PRESS

FAIRFIELD, WASHINGTON

1973

Library of Congress Cataloging in Publication Data

Jones, David, 1736-1820.

    A journal of two visits made to some nations of Indians on the west side of the River Ohio, in the years 1772 and 1773.

    Reprint, with a new introd., of the 1865 ed. printed for J. Sabin, New York, which was issued as no. 2 of Sabin's reprints.

    1. OhioValley - Description and travel.   2. Indians of North America - Ohio Valley 3. Shawnee Indians. 4. Jones, David, 1736-1820. I. Title. II. Series: Sabin's reprints, no. 2.

F517.J76   1973   917.7   73-7878
ISBN 0-87770-087-7

ISBN 0-87770-087-7

INTRODUCTION

Joseph Sabin, who spent all of his working life with books. as an author, dealer, bibliographer, and auctioneer, was born December 5 (?), 1821, at Braunston, Northamptonshire; England. He attended school at Braunston and later at Oxford but was never a student at the university as he was apprenticed as a bookbinder to Charles Richards, a book dealer in Oxford. His employer soon realized that he had an unusual young man in his employ and the apprenticeship contract was terminated and young Sabin was transfered to book selling. He was later made general manager and was in charge of buying books. A change was made in 1842 when he entered into a partnership with a Mr. Winterborn, book sellers and book auctioneers. In 1842 he married his partner's sister. The association of Sabin and Winterborn seems to have been successful but Sabin sold his interest in 1848 and sailed for America with his wife and two small sons. After a brief stay in New York he moved to Philadelphia where he worked for George S. Appleton, a bookseller located at 148 Chestnut Street, here he introduced a style of halfbinding in calf and morocco, previously unknown in America and presumably work he had learned in the Richards shop in Oxford. In 1850 Sabin returned to New York where he was employed by Cooley and Keese, book auctioneers located at 191 Broadway. Later he worked for Bangs, Brothers and Co., located at 13 Park Row, where he continued until 1856 when he left to establish his own bookstore on Canal Street, New York City. In 1857 he relocated in Philadelphia where his book business prospered for several years selling books chiefly to southerners. The outbreak of the Civil War brought this business to an abrupt halt and it seemed necessary to move again to New York where he established a book auction firm with H. A. Jennings. This firm continued until 1865 when Sabin bought out Michael Nunan's book business and once more established his own firm, known as J. Sabin & Sons, located at 64 Nassau Street. The new Sabin firm seems to have been busy and prosperous and it was here that work got under way for the monumental *Bibliotheca Americana,* or as the title page reads, *Dictionary of Books Relating to America, From its Discovery to the Present Time.* It is by this work that Joseph Sabin is best known today as he died more than 90 years ago, June 5, 1881, and his bookstore on Nassau Street is all but forgotten. The Sabin Dictionary was indeed a tremendous undertaking. Here the effort was made to list every book pertaining to the history of America. The Sabin work is in 29 volumes, divided into 172 parts, and listing 106,413 entries, however some titles were published in several editions so it is estimated that a quarter of a million editions are listed. In addition the locations in libraries of many rare books are given so nearly one million copies are listed in this manner. A work of this magnitude, issued in so many volumes and over a period of 70 years, from 1867 to 1936, cannot be free from minor errors. The Sabin Dictionary is not always correct, exhaustive, definitive, but it is indeed a tremendous book list and one which is still used extensively by librarians and antiquarian book dealers. It is still in print in the 29 volume form for a price of $445.00 and there is a two volume printing of Sabin in a greatly reduced type size which has a price of $95.00 Up to the time of Sabin's death in 1881 some 80 parts had been printed with 58,796 entries. Two additional parts were in preparation at the time of the author's death and these were published by Wilberforce Eames, then a young bookseller in Brooklyn. Working rather slowly Mr. Eames reached entry number 82,714 in 1892 and there the work got stalled. It was not until 1929 that more volumes were published, still under the editorship of the durable Wilberforce Eames, who got to entry 84,556. After this point R. W. G. Vail became editor and with the help of a staff of assistants brought the Sabin bibliography to completion in 1936.

While Joseph Sabin is best known by the monumental bibliography which carries his name he did have other accomplishments. In 1869 he launched a periodical *The American Bibliopolist,* devoted to book selling. This ran through 86 volumes from January, 1869 to April 1877. Although devoted largely to the interests of J. Sabin & Sons it did include advertisements placed by other book dealers and book auction houses and the non-advertising pages include much information on rare books sold in America in those years. Joseph Sabin seems to have died a poor man, improverished by his efforts to get the Sabin Dictionary in print. This was however not his only publishing venture for in the 1860's and1870's he brought out a series of historical reprints. These were tastefully printed and are still respected in the book trade where they turn up occasionally more than a century later. The Sabin reprints were divided into two series, quarto and octavo, and titles in each series were available in two states, large paper and small paper.

We list the following.

In the octavo series:

The Journal of Major George Washington, large paper 3.00; small paper 1.50

A Journal of Two Visits Made to Some Nations of Indians on the West Side of the River Ohio, in the Years 1772 and 1773, by David Jones, Burlington; MDCCLXXIV, large paper 5.00; small paper 2.50

Vindication of the Captors of Major Andre, by Egbert Benson, New York, 1817, large paper 4.00,; small paper 2.00

A Brief State of the Province of Pennsylvania, large paper 2.50; small paper 1.25

The Present State of Virginia, by Hugh Jones, large paper 8.00; small paper 4.00

The History of the First Discovery and Settlement of Virginia, by William Smith, The Narrative of Colonel David Fanning, Richmond, Va., 1861, large paper 10.00 small paper 5.00

The quarto series includes:

An Account of the Late Revolution in New England, by Nathaniel Byfield, large paper 4.00; small paper 2.00

A Relation of Maryland, large paper 8.00; small paper 4.00

A Farther Discovery of the Present State of the Indians in New England, 1661, large paper 5.00; small paper 2.50

Certain Inducements to Well Minded People, large paper 2.00; small paper 1.00

Strength out of Weakness, large paper 5.00; small paper 2.50

A Further Manifestation of the Progress of the Gospel Among the Indians, large paper 2.50; small paper 1.50

New England's First Fruits, large paper 3.00; small paper 1.50

Further Queries Upon the Present State of the New-English Affairs, large paper 2.00; small paper 1.00

The Day Breaking, large paper 4.00; small paper 2.00

The Clear Sunshine of the Gospel, by Thomas Shepard, large paper 5.00; small paper 2.50

There were also some later Sabin reprints, including *A Journal of the Late Actions of the French at Canada,* by Nicolas Beyard and Charles Lodovick, printed originally in London in 1693.

The Sabin edition sold for 4.50 in large paper and 2.50 in small paper. There was also a rare Virginia booklet, *Nova Britannia*, published in London in 1609, which Sabin sold in various states with prices ranging from 5.00 to 17.50. The above listing of Sabin reprints is probably incomplete but will give some information on the publishing efforts of this unusual man.

The original 1774 printing of David Jones is now of course a rare book. The 1865 Sabin printing of the David Jones work has sold up to $45.00 on the used book market.

Glen Adams
Fairfield, Washington
May, 1973.

A

JOURNAL

OF

TWO VISITS MADE TO SOME NATIONS OF IN-DIANS ON THE WEST SIDE OF THE RIVER OHIO, IN THE YEARS 1772 AND 1773.

BY THE

REV. DAVID JONES,

MINISTER OF THE GOSPEL AT FREEHOLD, IN NEW JERSEY.

WITH A

BIOGRAPHICAL NOTICE OF THE AUTHOR,

BY

HORATIO GATES JONES, A. M.,

CORRESPONDING SECRETARY HISTORICAL SOCIETY OF PENNSYLVANIA.

NEW YORK:

REPRINTED FOR JOSEPH SABIN.

1865.

PIOGRAPHICAL SKETCH.

———◆———

THE Reverend David Jones was a son of Morgan and Eleanor Evans Jones, and was born in White Clay Creek Hundred, Newcastle County, Delaware, May 12th, 1736. His father was a native of the Principality of Wales, and was descended from the famous Morgan ap Ryddarch. The early life of David was devoted to agricultural pursuits, and he lived in the midst of a population who were chiefly emigrants from Wales, so that he acquired the Welsh language; but in after life he forgot it.

On the 6th of May, 1758, he was baptized, and became a member of the Welsh Tract Baptist Church. Soon after this, he went to the Hopewell Academy, in Hunterdon County, N. J., which was established by the Rev. Isaac Eaton. Here he learned Latin and Greek, and made the acquaintance of James Manning, afterwards the first President of Rhode Island College, and many others who became distinguished both in Church and State.

Having

Having finifhed his ftudies, he returned home, and in 1761 he was licenfed to preach the gofpel by the Welfh Tract Church, and the fame year he went to Middletown, N. J., to ftudy divinity under the learned Abel Morgan, who was the paftor of the Middletown Church and a coufin of Mr. Jones. He was ordained at Freehold, Monmouth County, December 12, 1766, and became the paftor of the church in that place. It was during his refidence here that he became ftrongly impreffed with a defire to vifit the Indians in the territory northweft of the Ohio River, and endeavor to preach to them the gofpel. As a preliminary ftep, he laid the matter before the Philadelphia Baptift Affociation, which met that year (1772) in New York, and his project being approved by that body, he received a certificate of his good ftanding as a minifter, with a view to the profecution of his intended miffion. Befides vifiting the Indians, he alfo had " views of fettling on the eaft of the River Ohio, in a Province under the care of Meffrs. Franklin, Wharton, Baynton, Morgan, and others." His firft miffion was begun May 4, 1772, and terminated in Auguft. His fecond was begun October 26, 1772, and ended in April, 1773, fo that he fpent nearly one entire year in his travels. The details of thefe journeys comprife the contents of the volume now republifhed, and form an interefting

account

account of the manners, cuftoms, language, and religious belief of a people now almoft extinct. One of his companions, while navigating the Ohio in a canoe from Fort Pitt (now Pittfburg), was the celebrated George Rogers Clarke, who has been termed " the Wafhington of the Weft."

The miffionary efforts of Mr. Jones were directed chiefly to the Shawnee and Delaware Indians; but they were attended with very little fuccefs, and he finally abandoned the benevolent enterprife, and fettled himfelf as the permanent paftor of the Freehold Church, where he continued to preach, with great acceptance, until the commencement of the Revolutionary War. He at once efpoufed the fide of his country, and his zeal and devotion to the American fide foon rendered him obnoxious to the Tories, who abounded in that part of New Jerfey. His boldnefs was proverbial, and at laft his life was placed in imminent jeopardy. Feeling that it was unfafe to refide any longer amid fuch a population, he removed to Pennfylvania, and became paftor of the Great Valley Baptift Church, in Chefter County. This was in April, 1775. In the fall of that year, a Faft was recommended to the Colonies by the Continental Congrefs, then in feffion at Philadelphia. The war had already begun, and regiments of troops were being raifed all over the land. Mr. Jones preached a fermon

mon before Col. Dewees's regiment, in the Great
Valley Church, in which he took high ground
in favor of independence. This was at a time
when but few dreamed of cutting loose from the
mother-country. The sermon was entitled "De-
fensive War in a Just Cause Sinless;" — it was
afterwards printed and circulated very extensively throughout the country. In 1776 Mr.
Jones was appointed chaplain to a Pennsylvania
regiment, of which Colonel — afterwards Major-
General — St. Clair was the commander, and
which was ordered to the Northern Department.
He was on duty with St. Clair at Ticonderoga,
where, on the 20th of October, 1776, while the
enemy was being looked for from Crown Point,
he delivered a characteristic address to the troops,
which served to inspire them with fresh military
ardor. He also served through two campaigns
under Major-General Horatio Gates, and was
brigade chaplain under General Wayne, in 1777.
At the Battle of Brandywine he bore a conspic-
uous part, and on the 20th of September, 1777,
he narrowly escaped death at the Paoli massacre.
On the 4th of October following, he was at the
Battle of Germantown. He accompanied the
army to Whitemarsh and Valley Forge, and during the encampment of the winter of '77 and
'78, he rendered many important services aside
from his professional duties as a chaplain. He
followed

followed the fortunes of the army during the remainder of the war, and had the unfpeakable fatisfaction of beholding the furrender of Cornwallis, at Yorktown, in the autumn of 1781. By his untiring zeal, and bold, uncompromifing fpirit in his country's caufe, he rendered himfelf a marked man, fo that General Howe offered a reward for him, and a plan was fet on foot for his arreft.

At the clofe of the war, he retired to his farm in Eaftown, Chefter County, near his church, and devoted himfelf to the care of his flock.

In 1786 Mr. Jones became paftor of the church at Southampton, in Bucks County, Pa.; but after a paftorate of fix years he returned to the Great Valley Church and his farm, in the immediate neighborhood of his old commander, Major-General Wayne. Meanwhile the Indian War was inaugurated in the territory northweft of the Ohio River, — a country with which he had rendered himfelf fomewhat acquainted in 1772–3. General Wayne was appointed to the command, and, in 1794, Mr. Jones yielded to the General's requeft and became his chaplain, and continued in fervice until peace was concluded.

His love of country was fo ftrong, that, in 1812, although feventy-fix years of age, he volunteered his fervices as a chaplain, and ferved under Generals Brown and Wilkinfon until the restoration reftoration of peace. It was during one of the frontier campaigns, when called upon to offer prayer, fo impreffive and patriotic were his words, that, at the clofe, the troops gave three cheers for Chaplain Jones.

During his retirement at " the Valley," he was not an idle fpectator of paffing events, but his papers fhow that his pen was bufy in writing to the Prefident of the United States and the Secretary of War; and the prefs of Philadelphia contains a large mafs of his contributions upon public affairs.

The laft occafion that he officiated in public was on September 20, 1817, when he delivered an addrefs at the dedication of the Monument erected. at Paoli, commemorative of the Americans who were maffacred there in 1777.

Mr. Jones publifhed feveral polemic works, and he alfo kept a Diary of his experiences during Wayne's Indian Campaign and the War of 1812 – 14; but that which will make him moft remembered is his Journal among the Indians.

Mr. Jones died on the fifth day of February, 1820, in the eighty-fourth year of his age, and his remains were buried in the cemetery adjoining the Great Valley Baptift Church.

An obituary, written and publifhed at the time, gives the following eftimate of him as a man : —

" In

"In fketching the character of this venerable
fervant of the Crofs, truth requires us to fay that
he was an eminent man. Throughout the whole
of his protracted and eventful life, Mr. Jones
was peculiarly diftinguifhed for the warmth of
his friendfhip, the firmnefs of his patriotifm, the
fincerity and ardor of his piety, and the faithful-
nefs of his miniftry. The vain honors of the
world, it is true, are not his; but, in another, he
has ere this received a crown of glory, and heard
the joyful welcome, 'Well done, good and faith-
ful fervant.' In the Army of the Revolution he
was a diftinguifhed chaplain, and was engaged
in the fame arduous duties during the laft war.
As a fcholar he was accurate. Poffeffing a mind
of fuperior texture, he embellifhed it with the
beauties of claffical literature, and the riches of
general fcience. The Fellowfhip of Brown
Univerfity in the year 1774, as a teftimony of
refpect for his learning and talents, conferred
upon him the degree of Mafter of Arts."

The original MS. of the Indian Journal is
ftill in exiftence, and is owned by his grandfon,
the writer of the foregoing fketch.

H. G. J.

PHILADELPHIA, *September*, 1865.

JOURNAL

OF

TWO VISITS

MADE TO SOME NATIONS OF

INDIANS

ON THE WEST SIDE OF THE RIVER OHIO,

In the YEARS 1772 and 1773.

By the REV. *DAVID JONES,*
Minifter of the Gofpel at FREEHOLD, in NEW-JERSEY.

BURLINGTON:

PRINTED AND SOLD BY *ISAAC COLLINS,*
M.DCC.LXXIV.

INTRODUCTION.

KIND READER,

YOU *have in this Journal prefented to your view my travels in two vifits to the Indians on the rivers Ohio and Siota; in which a defcription is given of this weftern world, as far as the towns of the Shawannee Indians, which are fituated weft of the river Siota; together with what endeavours were made to civilize the* Heathens, *and my judgment on that fubject. It cannot be expected that a particular narrative of the occurrences of every day fhould be given, becaufe this would render the work voluminous, and too expenfive; but remarks are made on whatever was thought moft worthy of notice. Perhaps it may be afked, what motives influenced me to undertake a journey attended with fo much expenfes, hardfhips and fatigue? By reading of the Scriptures it appeared, that the gofpel is to be preached to all nations, and that fome out of all fhall join in the praifes of the Lamb of GOD: feeing but little figns of the kingdom of CHRIST among us, it was thought that it might be the day of GOD's mercy and vifitation of thefe* neglected *favage nations. And notwithftanding* notwithſtanding the diſcouragments met with, I am not yet convinced but ſomething might be done for their good, if the attempt was ſuitably countenanced. Thoughts relative to this ſubject have been in my mind for ſeveral years paſt, and at times with an ardent deſire to try what might be done ; but my circumſtances prevented any attempts till the beginning of the ſummer Anno Domini 1772; when, in company with Mr. John Holmes who travelled for his health, I began my firſt tour, and returned from my ſecond on the laſt of April 1773; containing the travels of one year lacking a few days, including the ſpace of near two months between my firſt and ſecond journey.

Concluding it would favour my deſign, and from a deſire to officiate in the miniſtry, without dependence upon the people, had views of ſettling on the eaſt ſide of the river Ohio, in a province then expected to take place under the propriety of meſſrs. Franklin, Wharton, Baynton, Morgan and others. This induced me to take a more extenſive ſurvey of the country than what otherwiſe might have been expected; conſequently am enabled to deſcribe this new world more to the ſatisfaction of ſuch as deſire to be acquainted with it. For the gratification of the reader, and the better underſtanding of ſome paragraphs in the following Journal, it was thought proper

thus

thus to premiſe a few things; believing that moſt readers will enjoy as much pleaſure as him that actually paſſed through the ſcene. It would be eſteemed as no ſmall compenſation to my hard-ſhips, if this Journal might be any means of exciting a pious emulation in ſome perſon better qualified to engage in the important work of civilizing *the poor* neglected *Heathens; and if any ſhould be ſo diſpoſed, cordially I wiſh* God *ſpeed to the ſame; and remain the reader's un-worthy ſervant in the goſpel of* Christ.

D. JONES.

A JOURNAL OF TWO VISITS TO THE INDIANS.

MAY 4, Anno Domini 1772, having prepared for my journey, and committed all to the diſpoſal of Divine Providence, went to Philadelphia, and converſed with meſſrs. Wharton, Baynton and Morgan concerning ſettling on the river Ohio; acquainted them alſo with my deſigns of viſiting the Indians. They all were well pleaſed, and gave me what encouragement was then in their power. Mr. Wharton was ſo kind as to recommend me to the notice of col. Croghan at Fort Pitt, as he was well qualified, from his long acquaintance with the Indians, to be of great uſe to me in proſecuting my deſign; and I underſtood that Mr. Morgan was ſo good alſo as to write to the colonel in my favour. Pleaſed with the preſent proſpects, left Philadelphia, and in order to ſee ſome kindred and friends, went thro' the province of Maryland, and on the 10th of May came to the chief

town

town of that province, situated on good navigable water, in the county of Baltimore, which is
also the name of the town.—'Tis a town of
great business considering its age, is connected in
trade with the western parts of Pennsylvania, and
appears in a prosperous state. I was there on
the Lord's day, and was favoured with an opportunity of preaching in the Presbyterian meeting-
house, the minister being absent. A number
of the hearers appeared genteel and very well
dressed; but was sorry to see the behaviour of
some so very unbecoming the solemn worship of
GOD—from whose omniscient inspection nothing can be hid. My hearty wishes are, that instead of whispering, talking and laughing, in the
time of divine service, all those persons especially
who are in an exalted station of life may always
conduct themselves on such occasions agreeable
to their genteel appearance.—In and near this
town are three places of divine worship, viz. the
church of England, the church of Rome, (near
of equal credit here) and a Presbyterian meeting-house, the last of which makes the best appearance. When I was there no Baptist meeting-house was erected; but several persons of
that persuasion were consulting to make prepa-
rations for one; and I have been informed that
a lot of land is purchased for that purpose. Set
out from thence May 14th; travelled on a course
of

of W. N. W. 60 miles, to an inland town in said
province, called Fredericks-Town; 'tis situated
on, and surrounded with good land, and a pleas-
ant country: and though it is so distant from
navigation, 'tis said, there are scarcely any goods
in Baltimore or Philadelphia, but what may be
had here, on almost as reasonable terms. This
town is much larger than what might be expected, perhaps owing to the frugality of the
German inhabitants, the greater part consisting
of that nation. In this remained only a few
hours, travelling from thence westerly to Know-
land's ferry on Potomack river. This river is
broad but not deep, consequently less serviceable
to the western inhabitants: it separates between
Maryland and the province of Virginia. The
first county adjacent to this ferry is Loudoun,
thro' this a tour was made, in which I enjoyed
opportunities of preaching, thereby gaining some
knowledge of the people and country. From
what I saw in that county, small encomiums suit
the most part of it. Indeed the country is well
watered; but poor pasture, and few good meadows, and many barren hills may be readily met
with. Within a few years past GOD has remark-
ably blessed the gospel here, so that it may be
charitably judged that many are brought to the
saving knowledge of CHRIST. Was agreeably
entertained with the truly grave aspect of religion,

ion, and cannot but commend that godly fincerity that appeared among the profeffing difciples of Jesus; though 'tis to be feared that
many yet remain ftrangers to the love of God.

Having fpent what time was thought expedient here, fet out for Winchester on Tuefday
19; croffed the Blue Ridge at Sniggar's gap.
Waggons do pafs over, but the mountain is
both fteep and ftony, which renders the tranf-
porting of produce this way almoft impractical.
The top of this ridge is faid to divide between
Loudoun and Fredericks county. Here we
croffed Shannadore, which is a ftream near 100
yards wide. Before night came to Winchefter,
which is the chief town of Fredericks county.
Near to this town, on the eaftern fide, is to be
feen the remains of a fortification, erected in
time of the laft war, and from its appearance
muft have been very expenfive: a number of
large cannons are ftill remaining on and about
the walls.

Wednesday 20 fet out for Fort Pitt. It was
faid the neareft way was by the fouth branch of
Potomack. Paffed this day over difmal ftony
mountains, the greateft part not commodious to
be inhabited by man. Lodged at an innkeep-
er's, whofe name is Murphy, about feven miles
from Rumney, which is the chief town of Hampfhire county.

Thursday

THURSDAY 21 come to Rumney, and there took breakfaft. This town is fituated on the fouth fide of the fouth branch of Potomack, and confifts of a few log houfes and a gaol; nor is it likely from its fituation that ever its appearance will be great. From hence we went up the ftream to colonel Haight's; moft of the road went along a narrow bottom adjacent to the branch; nor does the land, in common, extend to any confiderable diftance fit for any manner of cultivation. When we arrived to colonel Haight's, we found him agreeably fituated, and may juftly fay that he appeared hofpitable, kind and courteous.

FRIDAY 22 fet out for Patterfon's creek, where I fpent the Sabbath; preached to a fmall congregation collected from the fcattered fettlement, which is along this creek.—Hampfhire is the moft northern county of Virginia, and when I was there no minifter was fettled in it; but foon after, 'tis faid, a clergyman of the church of England arrived.

MONDAY 25 from Mr. Johnfon's proceeded on our way. This day paffed the north branch of Potomack, which is the northern bounds of Virginia. The road is cut along the declivity of a mountain, and the defcent exceeds moft to be feen ufed as a road. This day we began to afcend that mountain from others diftinguifhed by

name

name Allegini. Foreigners are much miſtaken concerning this mountain, for it is commonly thought that we aſcend from one part till near the middle we arrive to the ſummit, and from thence deſcend to the foot—whereas in aſcending we are near as high in going ten miles, as in any part of it. This mountain is truly worth notice, great part of which abounds with excellent timber; in general either oak, cheſnut or white pine, variegated according to the nature of the ſoil. That part of it called Savage Mountain is beautifully covered with ſtately white pines, which promiſe great advantage to the weſtern colony in proceſs of time. In paſſing this mountain we croſs many cryſtal ſtreams, the principal are called the Little and Great Croſſings. The firſt of which is between 15 and 20 yards wide, and the other about 60 at Mr. Hoagland's: with more propriety theſe ſtreams are called Little and Great Yochogini. They unite and empty themſelves into Monongehela, ſouth of the place where general Bradock was defeated: the Laurel Hill is about ten miles wide, and is only the weſtern part of the ſame mountain; but one reaſon why it is ſpoken of as a diſtinct place may be, the level land lying eaſtward, in breadth near ten miles: in this are ſituated the Great Meadows where Waſhington was defeated; the intrenchment uſed on that occaſion yet appears.

THIS

THIS mountain * runs a fouth wefterly courfe, and is at prefent inhabited in many places. Tho' part of the foil is fo cold and fubject to frofts, that little grain can be expected; yet it is faid that grain of all forts is produced on the Great Croffings. In moft places the foil is good for grafs and meadows. 'Tis very probable that it alfo abounds with various mines, and if fo, it will be of great utility to the adjacent colonies. It is faid to be fixty miles acrofs it, as we travel from Fort Cumberland to Redftone. Thro' the whole as you travel, may lodge every night in fome kind of houfes; but the entertainment is a little rough, for fuch as are but ftrangers to the new country. In this an amendment may be juftly expected, for a number of frugal and civil people are preparing good accommodations, both for man and horfe. When we defcend the Laurel Hill, which is both fteep and ftony, we come into that country which is known in diftant places by the name of Redftone. This name cannot properly be applied to the greater part ot this land, for Redftone is a creek, and the land adjacent makes a very fmall part of that country. This fettlement abounds with more creeks than can properly

* The whole hilly country called the Allegini Mountain is faid to run a fouth weft courfe, and terminates between South Carolina and Miffiffipi.

3

properly be mentioned here. Thefe all empty
into the river commonly called Monongehela,
the proper name of which, according to the
Indian pronunciation, is *Mehmonawangehelak*,
which fignifies, FALLING IN BANK RIVER.
From the richnefs of the foil, the banks of this
river frequently break, and fall into the ftream;
hence it takes its name. This river comes from
the fouth, and fixty miles before it arrives to
Fort Pitt, it is 200 yards wide. Several ferries are
kept on it, tho' it may frequently be rode in the
fummer feafon. On each fide of this river, along
the creeks, are fettlements amounting to many
thoufand inhabitants in the whole.—In this
country preached at feveral places, and made
known my purpofe to vifit the Indians. Met
with an interpreter here well qualified to fpeak
the Delaware's language; his name is David
Owens: agreed with him to interpret for five
pounds per month—the wages may feem high,
but none who are well qualified will engage for
lefs. He informed me, that it was neceffary to
fend an ambaffador before us, to know if our
vifit would be acceptable. This appeared rea-
fonable, therefore employed an Indian who lived
with him to carry a fpeech and letter to the king
and chiefs of the Delaware Indians. In this new
fettlement feveral houfes for worfhip are already
erected, one Baptift church conftituted, to which

I

I adminiftered the Lord's fupper. It was truly pleafing to behold the worfhip of GOD here, in a land fo lately overfpread with heathenifh darknefs and univerfal ignorance of GOD. Who could have expected fuch a change! but all things are poffible with GOD! May we not hope to fee the time when the knowledge of him fhall cover the whole earth! It has been his will to favour this new world with a day of divine power, in which it is hoped, a number are brought to the knowledge of CHRIST; nor has he left them without minifterial fupplies. The reverend Ifaac Sutton, a man of an amiable character, is an ordained minifter among them. Befides him, at fome diftance there are three candidates for the miniftry, whofe names are meff. John Corbly, John Swinglar and John Whitticur. Was favoured with an opportunity of hearing each; their gifts appeared ufeful for the edification of the church of CHRIST. The country along Monongehela is very fertile, exceeding moft to be met with in the eaftern colonies. It is certain that part of it is too rich for wheat, though other parts produce it tolerably well. Corn and potatoes are raifed to admiration. A perfon of credit at Muddy Creek faid, that one large potatoe cut into feveral pieces produced the firft year one bufhel and an half; the fecond year the return was fixty-four bufhels; neither was any dung ufed, uſed, for the earth is ſufficiently ſtrong without it. The timber, which conſiſts of black and white oak, walnut and wild cherry, indicates the fertility of the ſoil.

TUESDAY June 2, parted with my interpreter, who agreed to meet me at the river Ohio; went on my way towards Fort Pitt; arrived ſafe on Thurſday June 4; preached by the way at Turkle Creek; took a view of the fort—it is ſituated where the rivers Monongehela and Allegini meet: from thence the united ſtream is called Ohio, which ſignifies a fair, gentle or pleaſant river. The Shawannees call it *Pellewaa Theepee*, i. e. Turky River. At this time the fortification was remaining, but ſomewhat impaired. Here were about eighty ſoldiers with one commanding officer. It is ſaid the erecting of this fort coſt the crown £.100,000 ſterling: by ſome orders in the fall, it was demoliſhed and abandoned. Eaſt, at about 200 yards diſtance, by the Monongehela, there is a ſmall town chiefly inhabited by Indian traders, and ſome mechanicks. The army was without a chaplain, nor was the town ſupplied with any miniſter. Part of the inhabitants are agreeable and worthy of regard, while others are lamentably diſſolute in their morals.—Went to ſee colonel Croghan; was received by him very courteouſly; next day dined with him; his habitation was then four miles

from

from Fort Pitt up the Allegini river—confulted
with him about my vifit to the Indians; found
him well difpofed, and willing to affift ; was
pleafed to hear the colonel fpeak on matters relative to religion. He was kind enough to make
me a prefent of a bear's fkin to fleep on, a belt
of wampum to prefent to the Indians, and 60
pounds of bifcuit to fupply me in my journey.
This I muft fay, that the colonel acted the generous, kind gentleman. Part of the time at Fort
Pitt, was kindly entertained by Mr. Aneas Mac-
kay, who is deputy commiffary here; have reafon to fpeak of this gentleman as the apoftle
Paul did of Onefiphorus.

TUESDAY ‡ June 9, left Fort Pitt in company
with Mr. George Rogers Clark, and feveral others, who were difpofed to make a tour through
this new world. We travelled by water in a
canoe, and as I laboured none, had an opportunity of obferving the courfes of the river. It
would be too tedious to give a particular account; it may fuffice to be more general, and
refer the curious reader to a map * expected foon
to be publifhed by meffrs. Hutchins and Hooper.
It may be expected that this performance will be
accurate,

‡ Here I parted with Mr. Holmes who returned to New-
Jerfey.
* By requeft of Mr. Hooper I take fubfcriptions for this map at
a piftole each

accurate, as greateſt part will be done by actual ſurvey. As Mr. Hooper favoured me with
the diſtances of places, the calculations are
theirs.‖—From Fort Pitt the river Ohio runs
about fifteen miles near a N. W. courſe; thence
near N. about 14 miles; then it makes a great
bent for about 20 miles running a little S. of W.
thence for near 20 miles S. E. to the place called
the Mingo town, where ſomĕ of that nation yet
reſide. Some of this town were wont to plun-
der canoes, therefore we paſſed them as qui-
etly as poſſible; and were ſo happy as not to be
diſcovered by any of them. From this town to
Grave Creek is about thirty miles, and the river,
taking the meanders of it, may be ſaid to run a
little W. of S. Met here with my interpreter,
who came acroſs the country from the waters of
Monongehela, and with him ſome Indians, with
whom I had a little converſation. This night
my bed was gravel ſtones by the river ſide.
From Fort Pitt to this creek we were only in
one houſe inhabited by white people. All the
way our lodging was on the banks of the river,
which at firſt did not ſuit me, but cuſtom made
it more agreeable.

SATURDAY

‖ Mr. Hooper told me that by a more exact ſurvey made by
him, he found the diſtance between Little and Great Canhawa to
be conſiderably more than is ſpecified in Mr. Hutchins's calculation.

SATURDAY June 13, moved to a creek by the Indians called *Caapteenin*, i. e. Captains Creek. This creek comes into the river from the weſt ſide, and is ſuppoſed to be about 75 miles E. S. E. from Newcomer's town, which is the chief town of the Delaware Indians. We encamped oppoſite to Caapteenin on the eaſt ſide of Ohio. Here were ſome families of Indians—we went over and converſed with them, and in the evening ſome of them returned the viſit. Mr. Owens was well acquainted with ſome of them, and let them know what ſort of a man I was. They all ſhewed reſpect to me; even when ſome of them afterwards were drunk, they were civil to me, and would take me by the hand and ſay, "You be *minſta*." Here we ſpent the Lord's day: in the evening inſtructed what Indians came over. The moſt intelligent auditor is called Frank Stephens. He could ſpeak no Engliſh, but in this point, was at no loſs when Mr. Owens was with me. In this interview, ſpoke on many ſubjects, and aſked ſeveral queſtions, among others, whether he believed that after death there is a ſtate of eternal happineſs and of miſery? he replied, this he believed—he proceeded and ſaid, " he conſidered GOD as the Giver of all good things; if he killed a deer he thought GOD gave him that good luck." What he ſaid on this ſubject raiſed my expectation, for we know

that

that man is more prone to forget the providence
of God, than his exiftence. While many things
were faid concerning God, he gave great attention. At this time I felt myfelf much diftreffed
how to fpeak fo as to make him fenfible of the
way and manner that we received the fcriptures
from God. At laft thefe ideas arofe in my mind,
which were communicated in words to this effect, viz. "Long ago, oh! very long ago: fometimes at one time, and fometimes at another time,
God had good men on the earth; and by his
great power, God did fo confine the imagination
of thefe good men, that at that time they could
think nothing but what God would have them
think.* And while they were thus under this
great power of God, they wrote the fcriptures,
which tell us all things that we fhould believe
concerning God, and all things that we fhould
do to pleafe him. This was the fame as if God
had fpoken himfelf."—This I muft fay, though
I have firmly for many years paft believed that
the holy fcriptures were given by infpiration of
God, yet never had before a deeper fenfation of
their exalted dignity. What a mercy is it that
we are thus directed of God! how awful muft
the cafe of fuch be, who either defpife or neglect
inftructions from heaven itfelf!—What was faid
on this fubject much affected Frank, who replied,
"that

* 2 Pet. i. and 21.

" that he believed long ago Indians knew how to worſhip GOD, but as they had no writings they had loſt all knowledge of him : yet ſometimes ſome of them tried to worſhip him, but knew not whether their ſervices were pleaſing to him or not ; " and indeed this muſt have been the caſe with all, had not GOD been pleaſed to reveal his will to us; for no man hath ſeen him ; but ſays the Evangeliſt, "the only begotten Son, " which is in the boſom of the Father, he hath " declared him." This brought to mind, what formerly had been quoted in converſation from a certain author, viz. " a philoſopher was demanded by an emperor to give an anſwer to two queſtions ; the firſt was, whether there is a GOD ? having proper time given to ruminate on the ſubject, returned an anſwer in the affirmative : the ſecond was, how to worſhip GOD acceptably? after due deliberation anſwered, that this never could be known, except GOD is pleaſed to reveal it himſelf." Seeing that this is the caſe, from hence it appears, how exact we ſhould be in all our religious obedience to GOD; and never deviate from the directions given us in the holy ſcriptures : for all additions, though under the ſpecious name of decency and order, muſt be an abomination in the ſight of GOD.*

By

* Luke xvi. and 15.

By this time we were furrounded by the evening fhades, and repofe demanded an end to the prefent interview—informed Frank, that it was the cuftom of good white folks to pray to God, before they went to fleep—that we were now going to pray, and would pray for him—and tho' he underftood not what was faid, yet may be God would give him good thoughts while I was fpeaking. With this we all rofe up to pray; the Indians rofe likewife, being previoufly informed by the interpreter. With a folemn heart and voice addreffes were made to God.—Was informed that during the time the Indians looked very ferioufly at me. When prayer was ended, Frank told my interpreter, that my voice affected his heart; that he thought I fpoke the fame way that our Saviour did when he was on earth. It is likely that this Indian had heard of our Saviour from the Moravians or their Indians. It was faid by Mr. Owens, that it was common among the Delawares, to mention the name of our Saviour: but the cafe is otherwife among the Shawannees. An anfwer was expected here by the ambaffador fent to the chief town of the Delaware Indians; but a trader having brought rum, all profpects of doing good by any longer continuance, were at an end; and the ambaffador delaying his return, concluded to go down to the Little Canhawa, to view the land. This

was

was near 70 miles below, and from Grave Creek to the Little Canhawa, the river Ohio may be faid to run S. W. but it is very crooked, turning to many points of compafs.

TUESDAY 16, fet out for the Little Canhawa, and arrived to it on Thurfday 18. This ftream comes from the E. and is near 150 yards wide at the mouth. Went up this about ten miles; found, though it was deep at the mouth, that the falls were fo fhallow, that our canoes were prevented paffing further. Went out to view the land on each fide, and to kill provifions. Mr. Owens killed feveral deer, and a ftately buffalo bull. The country here is level, and the foil not defpifable, though not equal in quality to fome other places. It is not well watered, confequently not the moft promifing for health. In feveral places the higheft land is well adorned with ftately pine trees; and yet the foil did not appear too poor to produce good wheat.

WEDNESDAY 24, fet out for Caapteenin again. On our way had fome bad weather; viewed the land in many places; foil generally good; level land but narrow; good fettlements may be made on feveral creeks; fome were well watered; fifh in great abundance; fome of which we were fo happy as to take.

TUESDAY 30, came fafe to Caapteenin. Here was an Indian fent to me from the Delaware's

town,

town, who gave intelligence that their council were not all at home—that they were confidering the matter, and in a little time fhould hear from them again. This anfwer would have been better underftood, had I known them as well then as now. Being indifpofed in ftomach, which frequently occafioned vomiting after eating meat, and this being our chief fuftenance, was reduced to great weaknefs, and was in much need of nourifhment better adapted to my condition; therefore moved up to Grave Creek, leaving there our canoes; croffed the defart to Ten Mile Creek, which empties into Monongehela. It was thought the way we travelled made our journey between 50 and 60 miles before we came to the houfe of Mr. Owens. The feafon was very warm; all except myfelf had loads to carry, fo that on the 2d day of July with much fatigue, we arrived to the inhabitants, faint, weak, weary and hungry—efpecially Mr. Clark and myfelf. No victuals was ever more acceptable than fome buttermilk given by the kind inhabitants, which greatly raifed my efteem of cows. Stayed at Mr. Owens's over the Lord's day, and preached to a fmall congregation. To recruit ftrength, remained in the fettlement, and preached next Lord's day near George's Creek on Monongehela to about two hundred hearers.

ABOUT this time a fecond meffenger came from

from the Indians, giving intelligence that some of the chiefs would soon be at Fort Pitt, where a more particular account would be given, &c. At this time many of the inhabitants were near a famine, occasioned by the multitudes lately moved into this new country; so that it was only through favour that supplies were obtained to make another tour in the wilderness.

Tuesday July 14, in company with messrs. Clark, Higgins and my interpreter, set out for Fort Pitt; and as it was sometime before the Indians would be at Fort Pitt, took another tour through the desarts to Ohio. Preached on the Lord's day in a cabbin near to a creek called *Weeling*, to about 15 auditors. In the afternoon having sent word, a few Indians met me, one of which was Frank Stephens. Having all set down on deerskins presented to us for that purpose by the Indians, addressed them on these subjects, viz. 1. The state in which God created man. 2. His fall. 3. The promise of a Saviour; his coming and sufferings. 4. The work of God in renewing our souls to qualify us for heaven, and enabling us to believe on the Saviour. On this occasion was very sensible of the great difficulties of speaking on such important subjects to these poor heathens, who were strangers even to the historical accounts thereof. After due deliberation spoke to this effect, viz.

" You

"You fee, my brothers, that man is now very
bad; he does many bad things; he has a wicked
and bad heart: but when GOD made him at firft
he was all good, all love. Then he loved GOD,
and loved one another. GOD faid to him, if you
will only obey me, you fhall always live in a
happy ftate; but if you difobey, you fhall furely
die, and be miferable. But afterwards man
thought, may be, he might be happy and not
die, even if he difobeyed GOD. Then he did
that which GOD told him he fhould not do. But
oh! immediately he loft all his good, and became
very bad, having no love to GOD, nor to one another. In this ftate GOD looked on him and
faid, ah! you have difobeyed, and would not believe me: you muft now die, and you deferve to
fuffer for-ever: yet I have compaffion on you,
though you do not deferve it, and will fend you
a Redeemer. After a long time the Redeemer
came, and fo great was his love for us, that he
himfelf in our ftead endured all the punifhment
due to our tranfgreffions, in order to make peace
between GOD and us. Now GOD faith that all
that believe on this Saviour fhall be happy for-
ever. And to prepare us for that happinefs,
GOD by his great power changes the temper of
the hearts of all that believe: then they love
GOD and one another. GOD takes delight in
them, and when they die he takes them up into
heaven

heaven to be for-ever with himfelf."—Some white people befides my own company were prefent: it was obfervable that fome of them were more affected than when they had been more immediately addreffed. By what appeared expectations were raifed; but thefe Indians had no further opportunities, being in time of the fecond vifit down Ohio with my interpreter.

MONDAY July 20, fet out for Fort Pitt; had a fmall path called Catfifh's Road, which led us through the country between Ohio and Monongehela; had the pleafure of feeing a large extent of good land, but few inhabitants; it is fomewhat uneven, but moft part habitable.—Came to Fort Pitt on Wednefday July 22; remained about fix days; had an opportunity of converfing with feveral principal Indians of different nations: they all fpoke very agreeably, and feemed pleafed with my intentions of inftructing them. It is poffible that thefe men were honeft; but am now fo well acquainted with Indian deceit as to know, that when they are among us, to pretend to love what will beft recommend them, is their common practice. Being informed that it was fome time before any further intelligence could be had refpecting my vifit: therefore wrote another letter to the Delaware king and chiefs of the nation, informing them, that I had been long from home; could ftay no longer at prefent; but

they

they might expect me out again in the fall.
This was interpreted to one of the chiefs, and
with it a belt of wampum delivered with a
fpeech. Was informed all were delivered care-
fully; but faw not the perfon in my fecond vifit.

July 28, parting with all friends at Fort Pitt,
fet out for the Jerfeys; paffed through the fettlement of Monongehela, preaching in various
places; came to my own houfe in the latter end
of Auguft; found all well, through the kind
providence of God, who doth always preferve
us through all the dangers of life.

Health was fo much impaired by the great
fatigue of this journey, that it was with reluctance a fecond was undertook; but fearing the
bad confequences of difappointing the Indians,
was refolved to proceed on all events. Left my
houfe and family on the 26th of October all well,
but alas! all of them I never faw more. My
parting at this time went fo to my heart, that it
feemed as if this journey fhould finifh my days
on earth. It was like death itfelf, but for my
word's fake would go: but had it been known
how little in reality the Indians cared for my
vifit, might have contented myfelf at home.

For the conveniency of carrying provifions,
and as a defence againft ftorms, went this time
in a covered waggon, in company with a perfon
defirous to fee the new country, with a view of
fettling

settling there. Our carriage rendered our journey lefs expeditious, and in the event proved confiderable lofs to me; for the axletree broke in the Allegini mountain, going down to the Great Croffings—parted with it on fuch difadvantageous terms, that about five pounds lofs was fuftained. Met with difcouragements alfo while in Philadelphia, for there fome money was expected to pay my interpreter, but none could be had, only one gentleman, as I parted with him, put three or four dollars in my hand. Some were fo good as to truft me a fmall fum in fuch goods as were neceffary for my journey.—It filled me with fome aftonifhment to fee profeffed chriftians fo unconcerned about the converfion of the heathens! When the Son of Man cometh, fhall he find faith on earth!

Messieurs Baynton and Morgan were kind enough to furnifh me with fome neceffaries for my journey, and it is hoped that it will not incur difpleafure to give credit for their generofity. We travelled fo flow, and could make fo little way over the Allegini mountain, that we arrived not to Redftone till November 17. A few days before me the Revd. John Davis came here, intending to go with me to Ohio. It furprifed me to fee him fo much impaired in his health. Converfed, and found him refolved to go with me, at leaft as far as Ohio. Endeavoured to diffuade

him

him from his purpofe, fearing the event, (which in time came to pafs) but could not prevail; therefore confented, intending fubmiffion to the will of God. When we came to the houfe of my interpreter, found that fome time before our arrival he had, in company with fome Delaware Indians, gone far down Ohio : he left word that I might find him about the Shawannee towns, or fome where along Ohio. This was very difcouraging, as I knew of none fo well qualified as himfelf to anfwer my purpofe. Excited with hopes of finding him, in company with Mr. Davis and fome more, fet out for the river Ohio; but by high waters, and bad ftormy weather, our journey was fo retarded that we arrived not to Ohio till Dec. 2. When we came to the houfe of Dr. James Mc Mechen, formerly neighbour to Mr. Davis, he feemed to forget his complaints, and his heart was exhilarated upon feeing his old acquaintance, and the river Ohio, after fuch a tedious journey. But alas! dear man, his time was fhort, for on the 13th day of faid month, he departed this life, and left me his remains to commit to the earth. My diftrefs was not fmall on this occafion, for materials to make a coffin, and a fpade to dig the grave. Was relieved by hearing that in a cabin at fome diftance ·there were fome fawed boards, and a fpade could be had in going about eight miles. Having got the materials,

terials, and affifted by a man a little ufed to tools, made him a coffin. Happily I had carried fome nails with me, fo that he was buried with fome decency. During the time of his illnefs, he was very fubmiffive to the will of GOD; and was fo far from the fear of death, that he was often heard to fay, "Oh! that the fatal blow was ftruck!" He had a complication of diforders, and all medicines ufed either by Dr. M⁰ Mechen or my-felf feemed to have none effect. When he drew near his laft, he was very delirious, and could give few rational anfwers, tho' he ftill knew me, and would always have me by him, till all fenfes failed. To compofe him a little, gave him a ftrong anodyne, which had fo much effect, that for about fifteen minutes he enjoyed the ufe of his reafon. In this time he told me, that he firmly believed the LOCALITY of heaven—that in a little time he expected to be with CHRIST, *and fee and know* HIM *as he is now known, and as he is not known.* He faid his faith in his Sav-iour was *unfhaken.* Then he made as humble addreffes to GOD, as ever I heard drop from mor-tal lips. Soon after his delirium returned, and never remitted more. On the 13th of December 1772, being the Lord's day, about an hour and an half before the fun fet, this great man took his final departure from this world of forrows. Alas! what devaftations and deftruction has SIN

brought

brought upon the human race! that the wife,
the reverend head muft return to duft! and can
we who are alive, love fo mercilefs an enemy!
forbid it LORD!—Mr. Davis, it is well known,
was a great fcholar, poffeffed of a good judgment, and very retentive memory. He had truly
a great foul, and defpifed any thing that was little or mercenary. In our journey he told me
one reafon why he left Bofton was, becaufe he
abhorred a dependent life and popularity: that
if GOD continued him, he intended to fettle in
this new country, where he could preach the
gofpel of his Saviour freely. His addrefs, in all
his religious performances was eafy, fweet and
pleafing: his private converfation both informing and engaging; though at times he was a little referved, yet it was only when not fuited.
And what exceeds all, I believe he was a humble difciple of our bleffed Saviour. In this
point, was more confirmed by converfing with
him in our journey, than what I had been in any
part of former acquaintance.

BEING confcious that poetry is not my gift,
yet as the following verfes are expreffive of Mr.
Davis's faith, thought it not amifs to infert them
here, as an epitaph to that worthy man, viz.

How learn'd, how fam'd, now avails me not!
By whom admir'd, or by whom begot!

Ohio's

Ohio's bank my body now confines
In safe repose, till CHRIST in triumph shines;
But when the last trump's alarming sound
Shall shake the foundations of the ground:
And CHRIST in full glory shall descend,
The rights of pure justice to defend:
Then in bright honour shall this body rise,
To meet my dearest LORD up in the skies.

THE remains of this worthy man are interred near a brook, at the north end of the level land adjacent to Grave Creek: about sixteen feet **N.** of his grave stands a large blackoak tree; on this the name of Mr. Davis, the date of the year, and day of the month, are cut with my tomme-hock. This is the present monument; but Dr. Mᶜ Mechen intended a tomb for him. He was the first white man buried in this part of the country, but not long after a child was laid by him. Here a *Baptist meeting-house* is designed, as the most central place in this part of the country. When Mr. Davis's death was known at Philadelphia, a young gentleman there, who had a tender regard for him, was pleased to publish his character in the publick prints, February 1, 1773. Having obtained leave, thought proper to insert it here, viz. " By advise from Ohio we " learn, that upon the 13ᵗʰ of December, the " Reverend JOHN DAVIS, A. M. fellow of *Rhode-* "*Island*

" *Iſland college, and one of the members of the*
" *American philoſophical* ſociety, died there, af-
" ter an illneſs of three weeks, in the 36ᵗʰ year of
" his age.   Having completed his education in
" *the college of this city*, he was appointed one of
" the maſters of the *academy at Newark* in New-
" caſtle county, from whence, upon entering the
" miniſtry, he removed and became PASTOR of
" the *ſecond Baptiſt church in Boſton*.   His
" health being impaired, he returned in the latter
" end of laſt ſummer, hoping to receive benefit
" from his native air.   A number of people in
" the neighbourhood being about to ſettle on the
" *Ohio*, he accompanied them, ſeeming deſirous
" with the *Reverend David Jones*, to undertake
" a viſit to *the weſtern Indians ;* but death ſtayed
" his progreſs!————————

      " THE *powers of his mind* were *ſtrong from*
" *nature*, but much improved by a *judicious ed-*
" *ucation and ſtudy*.   He was *a clear reaſoner*,
" which faculty was much aſſiſted by his favour-
" ite purſuit, *the mathematicks ;* not deficient in
" *genius*, he reliſhed, with more than common
" ſatisfaction, the *writings of antiquity*, and the
" moſt ingenious of *the preſent age*. He was an
" *entertaining companion ;* poſſeſſed of uncom-
" mon calmneſs of temper.   In *his preaching*,
" he endeavoured to reach the *underſtanding* of
" his audience.   Educated in the genuine prin-
                                          " ciples

" ciples of *liberty*, he felt with the keeneſt ſenſi-
" bility for the *oppreſſed*. And when his *duty*
" called him, with a *manly and virtuous bold-*
" *neſs* defended them. A ſhort life can afford
" but few opportunities for *publick aêtion*, but
" when we find a *youth* ſtanding forth a *cham-*
" *pion of the common rights of humanity*, the
" reverence due to worthy charaêters demands
" our teſtimony in *his* behalf, whilſt we lament
" *our* loſs."

No ſcene of life paſt at that time more affeêted
me than the death of Mr. Davis; but ſince that,
met with ſomething that touched my ſoul more
to the life, as will appear at the cloſe of this journal. At this time my health was greatly impaired, and now having loſt my good friend,
had thoughts of returning home. While ruminating on this ſubjeêt, a canoe came along bound
for the Shawannee towns. It partly belonged
to Mr. John Irwine, an Indian trader, with
whom I was acquainted. It was 60 feet in
length, and at leaſt 3 feet in breadth; fitted out
with ſix hands and deeply loaden. The name
of the chief hand is James Kelly, who offered
to take me along. Reſolved to go, ſuppoſing
that travelling by water might be a means of re-
ſtoring health; hoping alſo that I might meet
with my interpreter.

DECEMBER 27, in the morning parted with my
brother

brother and other friends, committing the event
to Providence; fet out in my voyage to the Shawannee towns. The weather was fnowy and
fevere, yet being lapped up in blankets received
no damage. At night encamped on the weft
fide of Ohio, and by the affiftance of a large
fire, flept more comfortably than could be imagined, by thofe who are ftrangers to fuch lodging.

MONDAY 28, the wind blowing from the S.
made the river fo rough, that moft part of the
day it was impoffible to travel. It is faid by the
traders, that the wind almoft univerfally blows up
Ohio, efpecially in winter, nor do I remember it
otherwife: if this continues to be the cafe, it
muft be of great advantage to trade on this river.
Perhaps it would puzzle the greateft philofo-
pher to affign a natural caufe for the wind's
blowing up this ftream in the winter; but it is
plain Providence has fo ordered it. At evening
Mr. Kelly concluded, that as the wind abated, it
was duty to continue at the oars all night : therefore we fet out, and it was thought by morning
we were about eight miles below the little Canhawa. This night was feverely cold—the canoe
was loaded near eighteen inches above its fides;
on this was my lodging. Though well furnifhed
with blankets, was afraid my feet would have
been frozen. It may be well fuppofed that
thoughts of fleep in fuch apparent danger were

not

not the moft pleafing; for moving a few inches
in fleep, would have made the bottom of Ohio
to be my *bed*. Many thoughts arofe in my
mind what might be the event: at laft believing
that GOD had a command of my thoughts in
fleep, and could keep me from dreaming or ftart-
ing in my fleep, committed all into his hand,
and flept without fear. In the morning found
myfelf fafely preferved, through the care of him
whofe tender mercies are over all the works of
his hands.

TUESDAY 29, the wind being contrary, travelled little.

WEDNESDAY 30, the morning being pleafant,
fet out for the Great Canhawa, paffed Hockhock-
ing, which is a pretty large creek, coming from
the weft fide of Ohio. Several creeks came in
from the eaft fide, fome of which were paffed in
the night; the land paffed in the day time in
general appeared good and level: about break
of day, paffed the mouth of the Great Canhawa;
this is a great river, that comes from the borders
of Virginia, and is faid to be about 300 yards
wide at the mouth. The land about this river is
efteemed very good, and it is faid the feat of government will be here; but perhaps the Great
Guiandat will be found beft for the metropolis.
The mouth of this river, according to the calculation of Mr. Hutchins, is 226 miles below Fort

Pitt,

Pitt, but his affiftant Mr. Hooper, by actual furvey, told me, he found it much more—traders
efteem it 250. This morning took breakfaft of
chocolate, ufing rum as an ingredient inftead of
milk, and feemed very ufeful here in the wildernefs, where flefh was our chief provifion.

THURSDAY 31, fet out for Great Guiandat.—
The river Ohio in general bore a S. W. courfe
and a little more wefterly: but it is very crooked
in many places. This day being fair and pleafant, we travelled a great diftance, fo that the day
following about 11 o'clock we paffed the mouth
of Great Guiandat, being January 1, 1773. This
creek is very large, and it is faid that it originates
from Clinch Mountain, which feparates it from
Holfton river; and, according to information, is
fituated weft of the fouthern parts of Virginia.
If falls do not prevent, from the appearance of
this creek, it may be navigable for a great diftance for canoes and fuch fmall craft. Here the
land appears charming and level, well fupplied
with fine blackoak timber; and was informed,
that it abounds with extraordinary fprings, efpecially about the branches that make this creek.
In this part of the country, even in the winter
feafon, pafturage is fo good, that creatures are well
fupplied without any affiftance. Here are a great
abundance of buffaloes, which are a fpecies of
cattle, as fome fuppofe, left here by former inhabitants.

habitants. To fuch as travel this country it is moft evident, that it has formerly been inhabited by fome people, who had the ufe of iron. I have been informed by fundry perfons, that up fome of thefe creeks, a pair of mill-ftones are to be feen, where it is probable formerly a mill ftood. Below this creek's mouth the bank of Ohio feems near one hundred feet higher than the furface of the water in common; fo that no place that we paffed, promifed fuperior advantages for a town, as it will always be fafe from floods of waters, and eafy for the inhabitants of the colony to tranfport their produce down the ftream. The mouth of this creek, according to Mr. Hutchins's calculation, is three hundred and eight miles below Fort Pitt; but fome think it confiderably further; and from Mr. Hooper's actual furvey, it is probable it may be fo. About thirteen miles below, paffed a ftream near as large as this, called Great Sandy Creek. According to information, on the heads of thefe creeks is the moft beautiful and fertile country to be fettled, that is any where in this new colony; would therefore recommend it to fuch as are difpofed to fettle in this new world. Here the inhabitants will not be *perpetual flaves* to fupport their creatures, for the winters are mild and fhort, being near the end of latitude 38, or the beginning of 39. Contiguous to this, if none in it, are the

famous

famous falt fprings, which are a peculiar favour of GOD in this land, fo diftant from the fea. Throughout this country in various places falt fprings are to be feen; but more abundantly in the fouthern parts, the water of which, if boiled, produces very penetrating falt; fome of which I faw myfelf.

IN this country alfo are to be feen alum mines, as the people call them; but fome of them, from a chymical experiment, appear to be rather a mixture of vitriol with alum. This country has its excellences as well as fome feeming difadvantages, among which the great abundance of ftone-coal may be reckoned as one advantage, efpecially in procefs of time. The black-fmiths about Redftone ufe none other in their fhops, and find it anfwers their purpofe well; nor is it defective for materials to erect the beft of buildings, for there is no fcarcity of lime-ftone, and excellent quarries of free-ftone. At Great Sandy Creek the river Ohio makes a turn, and runs for many miles near due north, and from thence to the mouth of Siota, its courfe may be faid to be S. W. and a little more wefterly.

SATURDAY Jan. 2, it rained fo that we were obliged to remain in camp: and tho' we ftretched our blankets, the rain was fo exceffive, that we lay foaking wet in our beds through great part of the night. No night feemed more uncomfortable

fortable than this, yet was not fensible of any damage received.

JANUARY 3, it rained most part of the day, so that part of us remained in camp; but others, being worse disposed, went out to hunt, though we were not in real want of provisions; it was so ordered that they killed nothing. Upon their return reminded them of their impiety, and that Providence prevented success. All that was said seemed only like darting straws against the wind, for sense of duty was lost.

MONDAY 4, set out for the river Siota, and about the middle of the day came to the mouth of it.—The Shawannee Indians formerly lived near the mouth of this river, but finding that their enemies had too easy access, they moved their habitation up the stream. The mouth of Siota may be more than two hundred yards wide, and was then very deep, occasioned by the late rains. It is said that the mouth of this river terminates the colony expected to take place. For some miles before we arrived to this river, mountains seemingly impassable appeared terminating in several tops, covered with pine shrubs S. E. of Ohio. These mountains approach nigher the river Ohio, till they terminate at the edge of the stream almost opposite to the mouth of Siota. It is said that there is a way to pass over rather below Siota; and after travelling

about

about fifteen miles you will come to a famous level land covered with good pasturage, and abounding with fine springs of water, inviting inhabitants to partake of the rich productions of Providence. This must be connected with, or part of the land described above on the branches of Great Sandy Creek and Guiandat. The name which the Shawannees give Siota, has slipt my memory, but it signified Hairy River. The Indians tell us that when they came first to live here, deers were so plenty, that in the vernal season, when they came to drink, the stream would be thick of hairs; hence they gave it the name.

ENCAMPED on the east side of this river, at a place called Red Bank, and indeed this is the first place in which we could encamp with safety; for near the mouth in floods the waters of this river and Ohio unite, covering all the low land; the two rivers for a mile or better running near the same course, and not far apart. According to Mr. Hutchins, the mouth of this river is situated in latitude 38 and 22 minutes; and as Ohio runs three hundred and sixty-six miles below Fort Pitt.—Traders call it four hundred miles, and from the remarks by Mr. Hooper it may be supposed to be near the matter.

WAS informed that this river has its sources towards Lake Erie, and that there is but a very

small

fmall land paffage between this river and the ftreams that empty into that Lake. This will afford a communication with this weftern world not much thought of; for it is faid goods from New-York can be afforded much cheaper at Fort Detroit, than from Philadelphia by land carriage; having only two *carrying* places, one at Fort Stanwix, and the other at Niagara Falls. This river is very crooked, but not very rapid; fo that men in canoes can ftem the current to the head.

TUESDAY 5, the water being deep, the men rowed the canoe about fix or feven miles, and were obliged to encamp—I went myfelf on land and killed fome turkies for provifions.

WEDNESDAY 6, moved flowly—fpent fome time in getting poles for the canoe—the wood ufed is called paupaw, it is very light, and bears a kind of fruit in fhape refembling a cucumber, but too lufcious for fome ftomachs. This night our lodging was bad, occafioned by rain.

THURSDAY 7, as the canoe was poled up the ftream, for the advantage of killing game, chofe to walk on land; but miftaking the way that the river turned, loft myfelf on the largeft walnut bottom that ever I met with before. After fome time, found myfelf miftaken—what added to my furprife, night approached, and the fun did not

fhine.

fhine. After ruminating on my cafe, and recol-
lecting the courfes I came, concluded that I
knew which way the weft lay; therefore fet off
and run over feveral bad places, till at laft the
top of a very high hill appeared. Exhilarated
with the view, with not a little fpeed to this my
courfe was bent; but before it was afcended far,
had the pleafing profpect of the river, yet was at
a lofs to determine whether the canoe was below
or above me. Went firft up the ftream, fome
times whiftling, and at other times hollowing till
difcouraged—then returned down the ftream for
fome miles, till I was fatisfied that they were
above me—thence returning up again, expecting
little elfe than to be left in this folitary wildernefs, with no provifions, and little amunition to
kill any: but while mufing thus, heard them fire
at their camp for me. Returned the report, firing as I went; but as the wind blew towards
me, they heard me not, though happily their
guns were always heard. With as much fpeed
as the darknefs of the night would permit, being
directed by their continual firing, at laft arrived
fafe at the camp, and was received joyfully; for
their diftrefs feemed greater than mine, left fome
evil had befallen me, and they fhould bear the
blame. This day paffed a large creek on the
weft fide of Siota, and feveral fmall ones on the
eaft fide.

FRIDAY

FRIDAY 8, paſſed ſome miles up the river, nothing remarkable happening.

SATURDAY 9, Mr. William Butlar, by an accident, having got part of his goods wet, was ſo retarded in his voyage, that we overtook him, though he ſet out ſeveral days before us. In company with his canoes, we paſſed a place where ſome rude Indians were, who had behaved inſolently to Mr. Butlar. Our canoe-men, underſtanding the diſpoſition of Indians, for their ſafety, made themſelves near half drunk, and as they paſſed the Indians made ſuch a horrid buſtle, that the Indians were afraid to moleſt us, as they ſaid afterwards.

I THOUGHT at firſt this was only an excuſe for exceſs, but was afterwards convinced that Indians are extremely afraid of any perſon intoxicated; for they look on ſuch as mad, and among themſelves in ſuch a condition are always for *killing*. Encamped this night near the croſſings of this river, and ſlept ſafely, though not without fear.

10 Being the Lord's day, but as none is kept here, moved up as far as a place called Kuſkinkis. It is common here to diſload ſome part of the canoes, and from hence carry the goods on horſes to the towns. The land here is level and good, and it is ſaid that the place takes its name from an old Indian of the ſame name, who uſed to winter here. This river comes much nearer

7

to

to some of the towns, but as it is very crooked, it makes the distance so great, it is judged expedient to disload part here. Near us were encamped some Indians, which were going to *Pickaweeke* an Indian town near to Deer Creek.

MONDAY 11, Mr. Butlar and Mr. Nailar concluded from hence to take part of their goods by land, on horses brought from the towns for that purpose. Being very desirous of leaving the canoe, as the season was now cold, requested Mr. Butlar and Mr. Kelly to intercede for me to obtain a horse from the Indian that was going to Pickaweeke.

I HAVE reason to esteem these gentlemen for their assistance on this occasion, for with fair speeches and good treatment, a horse was granted to me ; but it is probable a large reward was viewed by the Indian, for they are very mercenary.

SET out about 11 o'clock, and came that night to Paint Creek, which is esteemed about fourteen miles ; the last part of the road is near due north. The Indian name of this creek is *Alamoneetheepeeca*, the English of which is Paint Creek. This creek takes its name from some kind of paint that is found in or about it. It comes from the west, and empties into Siota, near where we encamped. The water is clear and beautiful, demonstrating that it originates from good springs. On some branches of this creek

creek are fituated fome chief towns of the Shawannees to be defcribed hereafter.

TUESDAY 12, having taken breakfaft with Mr.
Butlar and Mr. Nailar, fet out for Pickaweeke
in company with my Indian friend, whofe name
is *Cutteway*, his wife and fome others. It may
be well thought that my journey was folitary,
for three words of the Shawannee language were
not known by me, and as little Englifh by my
fellow-traveller ; fo that we could converfe none
by the way. The day being cold induced us to
ride faft, fo that about two o'clock we came to
the town. About one mile from the town my
Indian friend caft off, and hid part of his load,
and leaving the women behind, made figns for
me to ride on with him. Perhaps the reafon of
his conduct was, left we fhould be molefted by
drunken Indians ; for when they are intoxicated,
their abufes are not confined to white people, but
they will even rob Indians. Drawing near the
town, many thoughts arofe about the event, for
to me it was not known that there was one white
man in town ; but all anxiety was removed by
feeing Mr. Jofeph Nicholas, a former acquaintance when at Fort Pitt. With kindnefs he received and entertained me with fuch refrefh-
ments as the fituation afforded. While we were
refrefhing ourfelves Mr. John Irwine came in,
and invited me home with him. Mr. Irwine's
chief

chief habitation is a small town, situated W. N. W. of Pickaweeke about three miles. By the English it is called Blue Jackets Town, an Indian of that name residing there. Before this is described, it is proper to take notice of Pickaweeke—it is situated south of a brook that, east of the town, empties into Deer Creek. It takes its name from a nation of Indians called Picks, some of them being the first settlers—the word signifies " the place of the Picks." Now it consists of about one hundred souls, being a mixture of Shawannees and other nations, so that it is called a Shawannee town. It is the most remarkable town for robbers and villains, yet it pretends to have its chief men, who are indeed very scoundrels guilty of theft and robbery without any apology or redress. Some of these took four or five mares from Mr. Mc Mechen on Ohio, nor was there any prospect of redress. Leaving this, went with Mr. Irwine to his habitation. This town is situated east of Deer Creek, and north of a large plain. This creek is clear and beautiful, appearing useful for mills and healthful for the inhabitants. The buildings here are logs, their number about twelve. This is a peaceable town, and in it lives *Kishshinottisthee*, who is called a king, and is one of the head men of this nation. The English of his name is *Hardman*.

WEDNESDAY

WEDNESDAY 13, Mr. Irwine invited the king
and some of his friends to take breakfast with
me, having previously informed him that I was
no trader, but was a good man, whose employ-
ment among white people was to speak of GOD
and heavenly matters, and came with that view
to see my brothers the Indians. None of this
nation ever saw a minister, except a chance one
at some fort; so that they have little prepossef-
sions only what are natural. When the king
met me, it was with all appearance of friendship,
and respectfully gave me the right-hand of fel-
lowship, with some kind of obeisance. His
friends that came with him he ordered to do the
same. When breakfast was ready, which con-
sisted of fat buffalo, beavers tails and chocolate
—in a solemn manner, acknowledged the goodness of GOD, desiring Mr. Irwine to acquaint
him with the design of my proceeding, and he
said the king approved well of it. In our con-
ference at breakfast, he desired to know my business among them, seeing that I was no trader—
told him that I could not give a full answer,
being a stranger to their language, and not yet
having got a good interpreter to speak for me,
but expected one, and then he should fully know
my business. At present told him only a few
things, because Mr. Irwine could not interpret
only in common affairs, not having long traded

in

in this nation.—Kifhfhinottifthee is indeed a
man of good fenfe, and by all that appeared was
my hearty friend. He was defirous that I fhould
inftruct them into the knowledge of GOD, but
he was only one, and there were many againft
me, efpecially at *Chillicaathee.* During my prefent ftay, vifited the king in his own dwelling,
and was always received kindly, treating me
with hickory nuts, which is part of their food,
being much fuperior to any of that kind in our
eaftern world. He is neither diftinguifhed in
apparel or houfe, that being one of the leaft
in town, being about fourteen feet by twelve.
He may be faid to poffefs fome degree of hofpitality—being much indifpofed one day, the
king's wife came with what was thought might
fuit a weak ftomach as a prefent to me ; the difh
confifted of pumkins which had been dried, but
were now boiled, and with it fome bears oil to
eat with the pumkin. As it was a demonftration
of benevolence, tho' my appetite was poor, yet I
eat a little. About this time it fnowed near fix
inches deep, and for fome days it felt near as
cold as winter in Philadelphia, though it is
thought to be about two degrees fouth, fo that
cold weather in common is not long. Before
removal from this town captain Mᶜ Kee, in company with major Smallman arrived. Mr. Mᶜ Kee
is now agent for this department of Indians, and

as

as his influence might be great, acquainted him with my defign. He appeared to be pleafed, promifing to do what was in his power to make my journey profperous. The Indians having told me, that my old interpreter David Owens was down Ohio below the falls towards the Waabafh river, therefore inquired of Mr. MᶜKee for an interpreter—he recommended one whofe name is Cæfar, who was a foreigner, and, as he faid, underftood fomething about religion, and therefore would be beft for an interpreter on that fubject—but was fo unhappy as never to fee him. We parted expecting to fee each other at Chillicaathee. It was with reluctance this town was left, before an opportunity was obtained to inftruct the Indians; but being deftitute of an interpreter, concluded to move to the chief town.

Friday 22, in company with Mr. Irwine, fet out for Chillicaathee, and arrived there in the afternoon. Here Mr. Irwine kept an affortment of goods, and for that purpofe rented an houfe from an Indian whofe name is *Waappee Monneeto*, in Englifh, often called the White Devil, but the word Monneeto is not of any certain fignification. Went to fee Mr. Mofes Henry a gunfmith and trader from Lancafter. This gentleman has lived for fome years in this town, and is lawfully married to a white woman, who was captivated fo young that fhe fpeaks the language

as

as well as any Indian. She is a daughter of major Collins, formerly an inhabitant of the south branch of Potomack, but now lives near the Little Canhawa on Ohio. Mr. Henry lives in a comfortable manner, having plenty of good beef, pork, milk, &c. His generosity to me was singular, and equal to my highest wishes. Soon after my arrival, dieted altogether with Mr. Henry; but slept on my blankets at Mr. Irwine's. By living on such victuals as formerly used, soon recovered my health, in a comfortable degree. Chillicaathee is the chief town of the Shawannee Indians—it is situated north of a large plain adjacent to a branch of Paint Creek. This plain is their corn-field, which supplies great part of their town. Their houses are made of logs, nor is there any more regularity observed in this particular than in their morals, for any man erects his house as fancy directs. North of this town are to be seen the remains of an old fortification, the area of which may be fifteen acres. It lies near four square, and appears to have had gates at each corner, and in the middle likewise. From the west middle gate, went a circular entrenchment including about ten acres, which seems designed to defend on all quarters. This circle included a spring. Mr. Irwine told that another exactly in this form is to be seen on the river Siota, the banks of which remain so high as

to

intercept fight of men on horfeback. 'Tis evident to all travellers that this country has been inhabited formerly by a martial race of mankind enjoying the ufe of iron, for fuch entrenchments, as appear in various places, could not have been made otherwife: but of this part of antiquity we fhall remain ignorant.

SATURDAY 23, in company with Mr. Irwine, went to fee captain Mᶜ Kee, who lives three miles about weft and by north from Chillicaathee in a fmall town called *Wockachaalli*, which fignifies Crooked Nofe's Place. Here the captain's Indian relatives live, and fome others. This feems only a new town, not having as yet much ground cleared. 'Tis fituated eaft of a creek, which I fuppofe to be a branch of Paint Creek. Some of the Indians of this town have a large number of the beft horfes in the nation; nor are they worfe fupplied with cattle, fo that they chiefly live by ftock. Captain Mᶜ Kee was very courteous, and ftill promifed well.—Returned the fame evening to Chillicaathee. The day following, being Lord's day, remained at Mr. Henry's reading *Sherlock* on revealed religion, which is a good book on that fubject, and may be profitable to the reader: but if the author could have vifited the Indians, he might have faved many arguments, and perhaps been more fully convinced, that without revelation there would have been

8   little,

little, or rather no religion among mankind. It is granted, that the apostle speaks of the Gentiles which have not the law, yet do *by nature* the things contained in the law, &c. 'Tis true that *nature may* direct to some parts of the second table of the law, which includes our duty to *man*; but it is far from being evident, that it directs to the first table, which includes our *duty more immediately to God;* nay, the scripture sayeth in this point, " that there is none that un-" derstandeth, there is none that seeketh after " God." * Had a deeper sensation of this truth, when amongst the Indians, than is common with us. In this town were near twenty white people, some at least of them were disposed to hear the gospel, but dare not preach without leave from the Indians; for tho' when among us they are lambs, found them *lions* at home. To be debarred from preaching on the Lord's day was very grievous, and made the day seem very long; nay, it seemed impracticable to attempt social prayer, for not a minute was certain to be free from the insults of rude heathens. How great is the mercy to enjoy opportunities of worshipping God without fear! yet alas! how many are insensible of it! and under all advantages, remain *real heathens* in practice; " how shall we " escape if we neglect so great salvation ? "

Mr. Henry has preserved a good conscience

so

* Rom. iii. 11.

so far in respect of the Sabbath, that he said, he always refused to work at his trade for the Indians on that day, and repeatedly giving them the reason, was so far successful that few applications are made on that day for work—the Indians now knowing when it comes. He told me they were not a little troublesome at first on this account, but by utterly refusing and giving them the reason why he would not work, they were reconciled. From this instance, am persuaded, if the traders were unanimously to refuse trading on the Lord's day, the heathens thereby might be brought into better regulations; but what is to be lamented, some of the traders are not concerned about conscience in this matter, and it never can be well accomplished except they are unanimously agreed. When I came first to this town, two of our canoe-men lay under the hands of an old *squaa*, having had their feet badly frozen in travelling from Siota. 'Tis likely they came with loads of rum by night, for if this article is seen, 'tis common for the Indians to rob them without apology. One of the men indeed had his feet very badly frozen. Having applied to me, let them know that what medicines were in my possession, were not adapted to the complaint, must have recourse to the productions of that soil; therefore prescribed the following poultice, which in a short time absolutely performed

the

the cure in a furprifing manner, quickly feparat-
ing the *mortified* flefh.   As it is cheap, and may
be depended upon in fimilar cafes, fhall communicate it for the benefit of fuch as are pleafed to
ufe it.

Take the frefh bark of faffafras roots, pound
it in a mortar very fine: then boil it a little in
water, mixing it up into the confiftency of a
poultice with Indian corn meal.   Apply it once
in twelve hours as warm as it can be endured.
Its operation is attended with a fenfation almoft
equal to burning, but this abates as foon as the
mortified flefh is feparated.

Monday 25, made a further inquiry about the
perfon recommended for my interpreter, was informed that he was hunting beavers, and would
not be in till fpring.   This news blafted all my
profpects of making an ufeful vifit, and having
no other remedy, applied to one James Gerty,
who was well acquainted with their language,
but a ftranger to religion; neither had he any
inclination to engage in fuch folemn matters, fo
contrary to the tenor of his life, having little or
no fear of God before his eyes: yet he was civil,
and, after much perfuafion, engaged to affift me;
but dare not proceed, he faid, before fome head
men came home, who were out hunting, but expected foon to return.   In the mean-time I employed myfelf in making a *Vocabulary* of the
Shawannee

Shawannee language, by his affiftance and Mrs. Henry's. Formed a method of fpelling this language from the Greek and Welfh. The (ch) is pronounced gutturally as Welfh or old Scotch, and (th) as Greek, by placing the point of the tongue to the upper teeth. Here *dipthongs*, *tripthongs*, nay, even *four* vowels are ufed in a word. Their language feems very defective in verbs; yet in feveral particulars very expreffive. At firft it feemed impoffible to fpell it, but cuftom made it almoft as familiar as the Englifh. They have only one fet of phrafes, therefore their language is commonly known by all. Having an opportunity here of exercifing reafon calmly, have a little changed my fentiments refpecting language. The ufe of words, is to convey the conceptions of the *mind* in fuch a manner, that others may know our thoughts; therefore the better thefe founds are known, the end of fpeech is the better anfwered. It would be almoft as rational to *whiftle* in company as to fpeak, ufing words *unknown* to the hearers. Was this well confidered, perhaps it would make fome of our fine *pulpit orators* blufh, who ufe as many unknown words in one fermon, as might *grace* a modern apothecary's bill of medicines. To demonftrate a little of the nature of this language, fhall give a fpecimen in their manner of counting to *ten*, viz. *cootte, nefwe, nethway, nee-eweech,*

nee-

nee - aallonweh, nee - cootwothwe, neeswothwee, swaasickthwee, chacootthwee, meetothwee. The common name for GOD is *Ouessa Monneeto*, the word Ouessa signifying good, but could find no particular signification for the word Monneeto. They call the Devil Monneeto; but when he is designed, the adjective *Mauchee* is prefixed. The word Mauchee signifies bad or evil: so that they call one the good Monneeto, and the other the bad Monneeto; this word is applied to a snake, and other disagreeable things. The chief men in speaking to me used another word, by which GOD is acknowledged as Creator, viz. *Weshellequa*, i. e. *he that made us all;* but captain McKee pronounced it *Coashellequaa.* Was distressed that my time passed and little done to purpose, consulted with the traders to meet for worship ourselves, and spend the Lord's day in the best manner we could among the heathens. It was agreed that on the 31st of January, should preach to the white people; the Indians were to be notified, that if any chose to come, they also should be instructed. Fearing the event, went to see captain McKee, who promised to come next day and interpret for me to the Indians; but he came not, nor is the reason yet known to me, not having had any opportunity of seeing him since: nor was the disappointment less in our town, for the Indians were so extremely uneasy, eafy, and ufed fuch menaces, that none dare meet; for nothing can be fafely done without their confent. They are arbitrary beyond conception of fuch as know them not. Ignorance often creates fufpicion, this is their cafe, for they feemed apprehenfive, that if we met together, 'twas only to counfel to take the town.

FEBRUARY 1, an Indian lately returned named *Othaawaapeelethee*, in Englifh the Yellow Hawk, came with fome others to Mr. Henry's to converfe with me. This Indian is one of their chiefs, and efteems himfelf as a great fpeaker and very wife: and this may be juftly faid of him, that he is faucy enough. On this occafion Mr. John Gibfon a trader, was my interpreter, being a man both of fenfe and learning. After common formalities were paft, he told me that he wanted to know my bufinefs among them; for he underftood that I was no trader. Firft, informed him from whence I came, and that my chief bufinefs was to inftruct them from GOD, for his mind was revealed to us, &c.—That I had a great defire for many years to fee my brothers the Indians—now wanted to talk with them, and was in hopes that he would allow me an opportunity. He replied that he thought fomething of that nature was my bufinefs. Then he proceeded to make a long *fpeech*, not with a very pleafant countenance, nor the moft agreeable tone

of

of voice, and replied to this effect, viz. " When GOD, who at firſt made us all, preſcribed our way of living, he allowed white people to live one way, and Indians another way ; and as he was one of the chiefs of this town, he did not deſire to hear me on the ſubject of religion, for he was reſolved not to believe what might be ſaid, nor pay any regard to it. And he believed it would be the mind of the other Indians." His thoughts were only natural, and ſeemed to have no other conceptions of my inſtructions, than as referring to the common affairs of life, conſiſting in living *like* white folks.

HE ſaid that they had lived a long time as they now do, and liked it very well, and he and his people would live as they had done. This Indian ſeemed like ſome among us, who conſider religion only as ſtate policy. And without doubt there is enough of ſuch religion in the world, even under the name of the CHRISTIAN ; but this affects not the nature of the religion of the Son of GOD, whoſe *kingdom* is not of this world, but is purely *ſpiritual*, which does not promiſe its avouchers *livings* and WORLDLY preferments ; but what is infinitely greater, it aſſures all that truly embrace it, that tho' in this world they may have tribulations, yet in that which is to come, they ſhall inherit *eternal* life. How often do we find it true, that the natural man receiveth

receiveth not the things of the fpirit of GOD. This Indian fuppofed that I would learn them to read, and faid it would look very foolifh for a man to have a book before him learning to read when old. In reply I faid, that fuppofe GOD gave us the right way of living at firft, that if any of us got wrong, it would be kind in the other to fay, brother, you have miffed your way, this is the road you fhould follow. Adding that he did not know what I would fay before he heard me; that he could not tell but what he might like it. And if he would give liberty, if I did not fpeak good, he might tell me, and I would fay no more. He replied that it did not fignify to make any trial, for let me fay what I would, he was refolved not to believe me. Indians can bear no contradiction, therefore by this time his favage foul began to be raifed. Finding that no good could be done by faying any thing more, for it was only making bad worfe; therefore as the weather was cold, and had no horfe, begged liberty to ftay in town till I could remove. This was granted with coldnefs.

HE faid, may be fome other nation might receive me, and I might go to them. From this time prepared for my journey, only waiting for good weather—for company and a horfe, intending to go to the Waindots; but afterwards thought it not expedient. Between this time

9   and

and my departure, was entertained by three Monneetoes, which fhall be defcribed hereafter. At prefent fhall give a narrative of the moft *dangerous* fcene through which I paffed.

SATURDAY, February 6, in the afternoon, was fitting on my bed in Mr. Irwine's houfe, and two of his men were fhelling corn at the door, an Indian lately returned from his hunt, came haftily in purfuit of Mr. Irwine's lad, who ran partly behind me. The Indian with violence feized him by the throat, and feemed to be feeling for his knife or tommehock. Seeing him fomewhat intoxicated, was furprifed. Putting my hand to his breaft, relieved the lad, and fpoke in the Shawannee language in the moft friendly manner. He feemed for a little to be pacified, but foon afked for fome tobacco, in the moft mafterly manner. Having forgot its name, told him in his own language that I did not underftand him. This enraged him, therefore he took fome tobacco, and with violence jobbed it to my mouth, faying *tobaac*. Told him that I had none. Immediately he was fo exafperated, that he drew a very large knife on me, and approached to make a pafs at me; kept him off only by the length of my arms, fo that he could not ftab me, defiring one of the men to affift me in fuch danger: but fo daftardly was his conduct, that he refufed to come into the houfe.

He

He afterwards apologized and faid that he faw not the knife. In the mean-time the Indian's mother came haftily in, and fprang between us, feizing her fon by the hand, and took hold of the knife looking fmilingly in my face, as is fuppofed, to pacify me, left fome evil might follow. By this unforefeen, and yet moft fea-fonable and providential means, got out of doors, and walked off pretty faft to Mr. Henry's, though I did not think proper to run—the dif-tance might be about one hundred yards. Can't readily defcribe my fenfation at that time. I felt fomething like to what you may call a *mar-tial* fpirit ftirring in me; my heart became void of fear: the great law of felf-defence opened to my view, on the frequent return of thefe words to my mind, " died Abner as a fool dieth ?" In cafe of another attack, was not without thoughts of ftanding up for my life, and according to my ftrength to repel force with force. But oh! how good the LORD is in time of neceffity to them that truft in him, in opening another, and much better way for efcape, as will appear in the fequel, without offering violence to the hurt of any one When that Indian befet me, had in-deed a knife in my pocket, but it was fo ordered that I did not once think of it at that time. Since that, efteem it a mercy from GOD that I did not; for had I made any attempts of the

kind,

kind, the confequence might have been very bad. This Indian's name is *Yattathuckee*.* Near night Mr. Henry was looking out at his window, and faw an Indian coming called *Old Will*. He knew him well, and defired me to keep out of that fellow's way, for he was afraid that he would do me harm. For concealment, went upon the cabin-loft, but it was fo low that if an Indian ftood with his back to the fire, and his face towards me, he might eafily fee me, therefore for difguife drew fome blankets over me. Prefently in comes Old Will, making inquiry for me, with terrible threats in fuch a rage, that he foon began to cry with venomous anger. Often he repeated, "Oh! if I could get one ftroke, one ftroke!" This was fpoken in Englifh—and Mr. Henry often anfwered him in Englifh, 'tis likely to let me know how matters were like to iffue. Mr. Henry in common poffeffes a calmnefs of mind, and on this occafion ufed it with great difcretion; he did not appear the leaft difturbed, but anfwered with an air of indifference, and faid may be I was gone away, for the Indians were fo crofs that he did not think I would ftay. Mr. Irwine, I believe, was not a little diftreffed on this occafion; and by his prudent conduct contributed to blind the *old murderer*. Mrs. Henry, knowing well the difpofition

* That is, a hafty fetting fun.

pofition of the Indians, caft in her mite, and by
what was faid Old Will defpaired of finding me,
confequently went home. But like Job's meffengers, one was not well gone before another
came, whofe name is Black Arms. He fpoke
only in the Shawannee tongue, I could judge
only by the tone of his voice, which was the
moft terrible that ever faluted my ears. His
voice was indeed as the very harbinger of death
itfelf, fo that every moment an engagement for
life was expected. But behold, through the
kind providence of GOD, a timely way of efcape
was provided. That evening a very noted perfon of this nation, called the *Blinking* Woman,
was at Mr. Henry's. This woman was fofter-
mother to Mrs. Henry in time of her captivity.
There were prefent alfo two or three fquaas befides. It feemed as if thefe faid fomething in
my favour, though I am not certain what they
faid, but 'twas foon perceivable that Black Arms
was quarrelling with them; the matter was
carried fo high, that it was evident the fquaas
would no longer bare the abufe; an apprehen-
fion of this made Black Arms very glad to find
the door, left he fhould have been roughly treated
for his infolence. During this time little could
be expected but death, yet as a fupport it came
into my mind that at our affociation my laft
requeft to my miniftring brethren was, to pray
that

that I might be dilivered from the hands of un-
reasonable *men*, which afforded me a degree of
hope, that GOD would hear their prayers, and
give deliverance in his own way. Indeed the
case seemed in some respects desperate, and was
almost similar to the condition of the Israelites
at the Red Sea; for if by night an escape was
made, the inhabitants were at such a distance,
and so many rivers to cross, that there was no
prospect of redress. But how infinitely wise is
GOD in disposing all things to unite for the
preservation of his people! When Saul and his
men surrounded David in the wilderness of
Maon, so that he was inclosed as a fish in a net,
behold! a messenger comes with the alarming
news that the Philistines had invaded his terri-
tories, which obliged him to return with all
possible speed. Wisely did GOD over-rule the
turbulent dispositions of this people for my safety; for the squaas, abused by Black Arms, were
friends to Old Will, to whom a complaint was
made of their abusive treatment. This exasper-
ated Old Will so that he resolved to give him
manual instructions for his conduct, for, said he,
" Black Arms is always quarrelling with women."
Upon meeting a bloody battle commenced, in
which each was so effectually abused, that they
were willing to remain in their houses till I left
the town. Who could have thought of such a
way

way to escape! From hence, have been induced
to say, that GOD often exceeds the expectation
of them that trust in him, and opens a door of
relief in a way unexpected by us. Before I
proceed to give an account of my travels to the
Delaware Indians, shall describe the *genius*,
customs, *government* and *religion* of this nation,
as far as opportunity and information allow me.
If any thing happens to be misrepresented, shall
make no other apology than it was not designed.

GENIUS.

THE Shawannees are naturally an active and
sensible people, not possessing a dull imagination
in some kind of sculpture or hieroglyphicks, if
the false faces used by their Monneetoes are of
their own formation; for nothing can bear a
much more shocking aspect. They are the most
cheerful and merry people that ever I saw—the
cares of this life, which are such an enemy to
us, seem not to have yet entered their mind. It
appears as if some kind of drollery was their
chief study; consequently both men and women
in laughing exceed any nation that ever came
under my notice. At the same time perhaps
they are the most deceitful that exist in human
shape.

As it is common to judge of others by ourselves, so these Indians, from a consciousness of
their

their own deceit, are very fufpicious of us having fome defign to enflave them. This made
me fare the worfe, for they furmifed that the
white people had fent me as a fpy. It is faid
of the Cretians, that they were "always liars,
evil beafts, flow bellies." Perhaps this may be
as juftly applied to the Shawannees. This I
found to be a craft among them, that when they
imagined any thing in their own heart about
you, they would fay fome one told them fuch
things, and all this cunning is to find out your
thoughts about them In common they are
men of good ftature, rather more flender than
the Delawares. Thefe, as well as other Indians,
are of timerous fpirits, far from poffeffing any
thing heroick, confequently they feek all advantages in war, and never engage without a mani-
feft profpect of victory. There is little danger
of their being faucy if there is not more than a
double number. 'Tis true that they killed many
in the laft war, but great part were timerous
women fcared more than half dead at their fight,
or elfe perfons void of arms to defend themfelves.
'Tis pretty evident to me that this will not be
the cafe any more, for laft war the fear of them
was upon us; but the LORD has changed the
cafe, for the *fear* of us is fallen on them, that
they are in almoft a fimilar cafe to the inhabitants of Jericho when befieged by the Ifraelites;
and

and from hence we may judge as *Rahab* did, that the LORD is on our fide, and will in his own time bring the heathens into fubjection.

GOVERNMENT.

THEY are ftrangers to civil power and authority: they look on it that GOD made them free—that one man has no natural right to rule over another. In this point they agree with our greateft *politicians*, who affirm that a ruler's *authority extends* no further than the PLEASURE of the people, and when any exceeds that power *given*, it may be juftly afked, by what authority doeft thou thefe things, and who gave thee that authority—whether in church or ftate? 'Tis marvellous indeed, when we confider human depravity, how Divine Providence has preferved this lawlefs people *in being*. But all things are poffible with him, whofe dominion is over the moft powerful animals and favage men. 'Tis more than probable that GOD has fome glorious events in view. Every town has its head-men, fome of which are by us called kings; but by what I can learn this appelation is by the Indians given to none, only as they learned it from us. The chief ufe of thefe head-men is to give counfel, efpecially in time of war; they are ufed alfo as moft proper to fpeak with us on any occafion, efpecially if it be important. They

have

have no laws among them to redreſs the oppreſſed: though they ſeem to have as much need
as any people, for they are given much to ſteal-
ing, both from white people as well as among
themſelves. Their cuſtom among themſelves is,
if any one ſteals, the ſufferer ſteals as much from
the felon as he judges ſatisfaction: and it is more
than probable that the ſecond thief has the beſt
of the bargain, for Indians are not eaſily ſatisfied.
In caſe any perſon kills another, there is little
ſaid, and nothing done; but if the deceaſed has
a friend, the murderer commonly falls a victim
to his diſpleaſure in ſome drunken frolick; and
it is likely intoxicates himſelf for that purpoſe,
for Indians have not much reſolution without a
dram. Mrs. Henry told that during her captivity, it was not uncommon for women to hang
or drown their children, when they did not like
them, and never concern themſelves ſo much as
to bury them. Nor were they guilty of this
cruelty ſecretly, for nothing would be ſaid on the
occaſion more than if a puppy had been drowned.
But ſince they became more acquainted with
white people, their conduct in this is amended.
Yet they are not all without affection.

CUSTOMS.

It is common in this nation to make con-
ſiderable lamentations for their dead, eſpecially

if

if they were perfons of note. They believe a
future ftate of fome kind of exiftence; but in
this their ideas are extremely low and fenfual.
'Tis certain that they think the foul of the *de-
ceafed* eats, therefore it is common for the fur-
vivors to drefs good victuals, and place it at the
head of the grave for feveral nights after the
perfon has been buried. They have their children in good fubjection: their manner of cor-
rection till feveral years old, is to dafh water in
their faces, or throw them into the brooks: with
this they threaten them on all occafions. They
have no form of marriage—the man and woman
agree for fo many bucks fhe fhall be his wife.
Natural affection feems very fmall. By women
beauty is commonly no motive to marriage; the
only inducement feems to be the reward which
he gives her. They have no thoughts of marriage joining intereft, every one afterwards having their diftinct property.

It is faid that women are purchafed by the
night, week, month or winter, fo that they depend
on fornication for a living; nor is it thought
either a crime or fhame, none being efteemed
harlots but fuch as are licentious without a reward. Poligamy is thought no crime—'Tis
common to have feveral wives at the fame time;
nor dare one of them feem difpleafed left fhe be
difmiffed. On the fmalleft offence they part.
It

It often is crime enough for a woman to prove pregnant, but this is not often the cafe, nor is it like to be while licentioufnefs and the *lues venerea* are fo common. 'Tis probable if there is no reformation, that in another century there will be few of them on earth. At prefent the whole nation of the Shawannees, according to Mr. Henry's calculation, doth not exceed fix hundred, including men, women and children: and from what came under my notice, this account is large enough. Among the cuftoms of this nation, their cruelty to captives, who are not adopted, may be reckoned as one fingularly bad. When a captive is brought in, if any in the town fancy the perfon for a wife, hufband, fon or daughter, then that perfon purchafes the captive, and keeps him as his own. But it often happens that the poor captive has no friend, then a knife is run thro' between the wrift bones, and drawing deer finews through the wounds, they proceed to bind them naked to the poft in the long houfe, and, inftead of fympathizing, make all imaginable diverfion of the helplefs agonizing captive. Sometimes they will come up and cut off the captive's nofe, and make abundance of game at his disfigured afpect. When they have finifhed this fcene, they lead them out, and with their tommehock complete their defign, often leaving their bodies to be confumed by the fowls

of

of the air. Oh! favage cruelty! Alas! how great is the depravity of human nature! are thefe defcendants of him, who at firft was made after the IMAGE of GOD? yes, verily; but the fine gold is become as the *dim brafs*. How abfolutely needful to be born again! and how great is that work of GOD's fpirit, to make fuch as thefe new creatures, as inoffenfive as doves or *lambs!* yet this has been the cafe.* This muft be the cafe when that paffage is more fully accomplifhed, which faith, "the *wolf* alfo fhall dwell with the lamb————the calf, young lion and fatling together————they fhall not hurt nor deftroy————for the earth fhall be full of the knowledge of the LORD."†

DIVERSIONS.

IN the winter feafon, part of their time is fpent at playing a game which they call Mamundis, but this is more common among the Delawares: their minds are more attracted to cards, which, fome white people fay, they have learned from the French. This might be only an excufe for their own bad conduct. They are moft indefatigable dancers, continuing almoft every night in the winter to near twelve o'clock. Their mufick is only a fkin ftretched over a keg —on this the mufician beats with one ftick. As

an

* 1 Cor. vi. 11. † Ifaiah xi. 6—9.

an affiftant another ftands up fhaking in his hand
a gourd, that has a parcel of grains of corn in it.
But as they dance, all fing, fo that the echo of
their united voices may be heard at a great diftance. Fifhing and hunting employ their men
in fummer, and raifing corn the women.

THE women are the only drudges, but in return poffefs the riches; for what in fummer the
men make, is chiefly given to the women for
their winter's lodging. Among their diverfions
their mock-devils are none of the leaft. Indeed
they may be efteemed as a great curiofity; and
fo fhocking is their appearance, that had not
Mr. Braynard defcribed them, fhould have been
more furprifed. Thefe they call *Monneetoes*.
Not long before my departure, three of thefe
made their appearance, in confequence as they
faid of a dream. Being premonifhed, went out
of the cabin, while they were diftant near one
hundred yards. 'Tis more than probable that
the Monneetoes knew me, and intended to fcare
me. The foremoft ftooped down by a tree and
took fight as if he defigned to fhoot at me: but
I could fee that he had only a pole in his hand.
Each has a pole in his hand to keep off the
dogs, which on this occafion feem frightened
almoft out of their fenfes. As they approached
their noife was fhocking, nor were their actions
to be eafily imitated. Each had a falfe face, and

all

all dreffed in bearfkin with the hair on, fo that the only refemblance of their fpecies confifted in walking. The foremoft had a red face, with a prodigious long nofe, and big lips; the others had black faces with long chins refembling bears. All had cafed tortoife fhells, with artificial necks —grains of corn are put into thefe, to make a gingle—and many other trinkets are ufed to complete the noife. With all thefe frantick capers I was by them furrounded—afked what they wanted? but Monneetoes can't fpeak. After fome time they produced a pipe, by which it was underftood that tobacco was acceptable. Upon the reception of any donation, fome kind of obeifance is made, and as they depart, the fcene is ended with a kind of dance refembling the actions of a bear. In fhort their looks, voices and actions were fuch, that it was thought if they had got their famples from beneath, the fcene could not be much exceeded. This apparel is ufed alfo by their pouwouers in their attempts of healing the fick, when they cannot find out the caufe of their diforder.

RELIGION.

IT is faid of thefe as well as of all Indians that I heard of, that they believe there is a good Monneeto and a bad Monneeto: but they in no manner worfhip either one or the other. 'Tis

doing

doing them injuftice to fay they worfhip the
Devil, for they give themfelves no concern about
GOD or the Devil. They have not one thought
worthy of GOD. 'Tis a fubject neither thought
on, nor fpoken of. In no way do they acknowl-
edge either mercies or judgments as coming
from GOD. They feem to have fome conceptions of his making the world at firft: but none
as a preferver or governor of the works of his
hands. Never do they call on any higher power
to interpofe in any diftrefs—neither do they
apprehend that he is difpleafed with any of
their actions, not thinking any thing to be a fin
—they feem to have no defire to know him.
'Tis faid, by them that are beft acquainted with
them, that it never doth appear that they have
any reproof of confcience for crimes committed:
fo that it may well be faid, that they are without
any kind of religion good or bad, inward or out-
ward. It would be a mercy if this reprefentation could be confined to the Shawannees; but
how many are among us that though they pro-
fefs that they know GOD, yet in works deny
him? There is much noife in the world about
what they call *natural religion*, but I am fully
convinced now there is no fuch thing exifting;
for if men had neither tradition, or revelation
other ways, they would concern themfelves about
GOD little more than the brutes that perifh.
'Tis

'Tis probable some may say, that some heathens have wrote well concerning GOD. This is granted, but pray, kind reader, how came they by that knowledge? had they no *tradition* to begin on? till it is proved that they had none, the argument is not affected, and this is a point that never can be made appear. Whoever reads *Grotius* on the truth of the christian religion, will see how they came by their knowledge. And whoever considers that the world was in a comparison then young, will see that *tradition* was not extinct.* Is it not a great crime to use the knowledge obtained from *revelation*, only to malign it? it is indeed horrid ingratitude. And are they not guilty of this, who call that knowledge obtained from it by the name of *natural* religion? it is wished that such persons could only see the Indians, especially such as have least acquaintance with us: for others gain knowledge from us, therefore if judgment is formed from such, a great mistake will be made by supposing that to be natural, which is acquired. 'Tis more than probable, if the experiment was made, that they would be so convinced as to give up the point, acknowledging that if GOD had not revealed himself to us, we would have never made it our concern to seek after him. We read noth-

ing

---

* By tradition is meant something handed down from Adam to Noah, and from him to his posterity, &c.

ing of Adam's concerns about GOD after his
tranfgreffion, 'till GOD firft calls upon him.
Might we not have expected to find him, who
fo lately poffeffed the image of GOD, breaking
out into a foliloquy fomething like unto this,
"Alas! where am I! to what a ftate has my vain,
my ungrateful attempts brought me! now I feel
nothing but gloomy darknefs overfpreading all
my wretched foul, and an awful diftance from
that GOD, with whom I was wont to have the
fweeteft communion. How can I thus live,
robbed of my paradife of joy! Oh! will HEAVEN
look down on fuch a rebel!" But the facred
hiftorian gives not the leaft hint of any *relentings*
on this occafion, nor of any defires after GOD.
And if the cafe was fo with our firft parent after
his tranfgreffion, can we expect any of his defcendants to be better difpofed? fuch an expectation would indicate both *ignorance* and *arro-
gance.*—Though the prefent cafe of thefe Indians
is fo deplorable, yet it is my opinion, that they
might be civilized in a fhort time, if it became
a matter of publick *concern,* and authority would
interpofe to fupport fome well difpofed and well
qualified perfons, who would be willing to endure hardfhips for the good of the needy. There
is one difficulty in common not confidered, viz.
this people live a vagrant life, feldom remaining
long in one place, efpecially in the fummer fea-
son.

fon. If they were perfuaded and affifted in farming, and learned to read, they might foon be civilized. 'Tis ftrange that nothing has been done by the provinces contiguous to the Indians. Under all thefe difadvantages, if there was no rum brought among them, it appears to me that fome good might have been done. Some have thought that the traders prejudiced the Indians againft me. 'Tis poffible that there were fome fo bad, but in general I muft clear them of the charge, believing that it would have been very agreeable to have feen my journey fuccefsful. Some of the traders were not only civil, but very generous: efpecially meffrs. Irwine, Henry and Duncan: the others were very kind, but had not an equal opportunity of fhewing hofpitality. I am forry that I was obliged to remove before more inftructions could be given in return for their kindnefs: but fuch was the diftrefs, that my beft friends advifed my removal, At prefent indeed it is not fafe for any perfon to venture himfelf among thefe lawlefs favages, who have no confcience about fhedding innocent blood.

I WOULD difmifs the fubject about thefe Indians, only it will be expected that fome defcription of their apparel fhould be given. In this refpect they differ nothing from moft of other Indians. The men wear fhirts, match-coats, breech-clouts, leggins and mockefons, called by

them

them *mockeetha*. Their ornaments are filver plates about their arms, above and below their elbows. Nofe jewels are common. They paint their faces, and cut the rim of their ears, fo as to ftretch them very large. Their head is dreffed in the beft mode, with a black filk handkerchief about it; or elfe the head is all fhaved only the crown, which is left for the fcalp. The hair in this has a fwan's plume, or fome trinket of filver tied in it. The women wear fhort fhifts over their ftroud, which ferves for a petticoat. Sometimes a calico bed-gown. Their hair is parted and tied behind. They paint only in fpots in common on their cheeks. Their ears are never cut, but fome have ten filver rings in them. One fquaa will have near five hundred filver broaches ftuck in her fhift, ftroud and leggins. Men and women are very proud, but men feem to exceed in this vice. 'Tis faid that they fuffer no hair to grow on their body, only on their head. Some pull out their eyebrows.

No company prefenting, and matters not wearing the beft afpect, concluded not to go to the Waindots, but to direct my courfe to the Delaware Indians; having got a horfe through the kindnefs of Mr. Irwine, which coft me twenty-five dollars: and being fomewhat furnifhed with provifions for my journey, on Monday February 8, about ten o'clock, parted with

my

my good friends at Chillicaathee, and set out alone, passing through Pickaweeke; came before night to Kiskapookee, which is situated on a creek that soon empties into Siota. The town is near one mile from the river.—This day's journey was more than twenty miles—the course near northeast and by north. For the first eight miles, was not without some apprehensions of being pursued, but after that, was very little disturbed in mind. At this town my lodging was with Mr. Richard Butlar, brother to William Butlar before mentioned, His usage was kind and generous, not only preparing wheat cakes for my journey, but he also gave me two pair of leggins to barter for provisions by the way; for these Indians as yet have not the use of money. In the morning my horse could not be found, and by that means missed of company: however about one o'clock passed over Siota in a canoe, in company with Mr. Butlar, who was so kind as to see me over, because I could not converse with Indians about my ferriage. The lad that brought me over is a white captive. When I spoke to him, was very sorry to see him shake his head, and reply, " *Motta keeno toleeh neekaana,*" i. e. I do not understand you, my friend. There remain a considerable number of captives in this nation, which were all to have been restored at the conclusion of the last peace, and

without

without doubt the *agent* has in this point been deficient. The country through which I paffed to-day appears very excellent, only it abounds very much with bogs, or what may be called frefh marfhes, fo that perhaps it may not be beft for health; but promifes to be extraordinary for ftock. My courfe to-day was about northeaft. As I paffed a certain place called the *Great Lick*, faw the laft flock of parrots. Thefe birds are in great abundance about Siota in winter, and in fummer 'tis probable they may be feen much further towards the north. Having fet out very late, night came on before I arrived to the next town. My road was very fmall, and the night dark in this wide wildernefs, made my travelling more difagreeable than can be eafily expreffed: but before nine o'clock, came fafe to Mr. Mc-Cormick's at the Standing Stone. This town confifts chiefly of Delaware Indians. It is fitu-ated on a creek called Hockhockin. The foil about this is equal to the higheft wifhes, but the creek appears muddy. Though it is not wide, yet it foon admits large canoes, and from hence peltry is tranfmitted to Fort Pitt. Overtook here Mr. David Duncan, a trader from Shippen's town, who was going to Fort Pitt.

WEDNESDAY 10, intending to travel forty miles, fet out early in the morning—our courfe more northerly than northeaft—the land chiefly

low

low and level—and where our horses broke thro'
the frost, it might be called bad road and good
land. There were no inhabitants by the way.
Before night, came to the designed town, called
Dan. Elleot's wife's; a man of that name was
said to have here a squaa for his pretended wife.
This is a small town consisting of Delawares and
Shawannees. The chief is a Shawannee woman,
who is esteemed very rich—she entertains travellers—there were four of us in company, and for
our use, her negro quarter was evacuated this
night, which had a fire in the middle without
any chimney.* This woman has a large stock,
and supplied us with milk. Here also we got
corn for our horses at a very expensive price:
but Mr. Duncan paid for me here, and in our
journey till we parted. About a mile before we
came to this town, we crossed a clear large stream,
called Salt Lick Creek, which empties into Muskingum, on which the chief Delaware town is
situated. The country here appeared calculated
for health, fertile and beautiful.

THURSDAY 11, set out for a small town called
Conner's, a man of that name residing there.

OUR course was near northeast—the distance
was less than the preceding day's journey, so that
we arrived to town some time before sunset.
Travelled

* This woman has several negroes who were taken from Virginia in time of last war, and now esteemed as her property.

Travelled this day over a good country, only wanting inhabitants. This town is situated near no creek, a good spring supplying them with water—the land about it is level and good, the timber being chiefly blackoak, indicates it will produce good wheat, if a trial was made. Mr. Conner, who is a white man, a native of Maryland, told me that he intended to sow wheat in the fall following, and was resolved to proceed to farming at all events. 'Tis probable that he will be as good as his word, for he is a man that seems not to fear GOD, and it is likely that he will not regard man. His connections will favour his attempts, for according to their way, he and the chief Indian of this town are married to two sisters. These women were captives, and it is likely from childhood, for they have the very actions of Indians, and speak broken English. It seemed strange to me to see the captives have the exact gestures of Indians. Might we not infer from hence, that if Indians were educated as we are, they would be like us? This town consists of Shawannees and Delawares; and some of them dwell in pretty good log houses well shingled with nails. Mr. Conner keeps a sort of a tavern, and has moderate accommodations, and though he is not what he should be, yet he was kind to me.

FRIDAY 12, here we parted with some of our
company,

company, whofe abfence was very agreeable, and
in company with Mr. Duncan, fet out for New-
Comer's Town, which is the chief town of the
Delawares. Had gone but a few miles till we
came to the Little Shawannee Woman's Town.
This is fituated on the weft fide of Mufkingum,
and chiefly confifts of Shawannees. Here we
croffed the river in a canoe, our horfes fwimming
by its fide. The country began to be hilly,
interfperfed with fome barren plains. We paffed
Captain White Eye's Town, but this noted Indian was down Ohio, perhaps with my old interpreter, fo that I could not have the fatisfaction
of feeing him this time, but I faw him feveral
times the firft vifit. He was the only Indian I
met with in all my travels, that feemed to have
a defign of accomplifhing fomething future. He
told me that he intended to be religious, and
have his children educated. He faw that their
way of living would not anfwer much longer—
game grew fcarce—they could not much longer
pretend to live by hunting, but muft farm, &c.—
But faid, he could not attend to matters of religion now, for he intended to make a great *hunt*
down Ohio, and take the fkins himfelf to Philadelphia. I was informed that he accomplifhed
this, and went round by the gulf of Florida to
Philadelphia. On this occafion, could not but
think of that text of fcripture, which fays, " one

went

went to his farm and another to his merchandife." And it may be faid, the Indian went to his hunting. This was the cafe laft year, and perhaps fomething as important may employ the next year, and fo the life of man is fpent, few remembring that ONE THING is *needful.*

A FEW miles north of White Eye's town, there is a fmall town, where we obliged our horfes to take the river, following them in a fmall canoe belonging to the Indians. Thence travelled over very hilly land till we came within two or three miles of New-Comer's Town, and from that to town the land is agreeable and appears good for wheat. Came to town before night, and found it was a great triennial feaft, confequently little could be done till that ended. From the great town Chillicaathee to this chief town of the Delawares, is called one hundred and thirty miles. The courfe may be eftimated near northeaft, but as the path goes, it varies in many places. This town is fituated on the weft fide of the river Mufkingum, which is a pretty large ftream. The proper pronunciation in Indian is *Moofkin-gung*, i. e. Elk Eye River. In their language an elk being called *moos*. This town takes its name from the name of the king, who is called *Neetotwhealemon*, i. e. New-Comer.

SATURDAY 13, was fo happy as to meet Jofeph Peappi, a Moravian Indian here, who is a good

good interpreter. Made application to him for his affiftance in fpeaking to the king. He engaged and fpoke very kindly on the occafion. He went and informed the king that I was in town, and would wait on him prefently, and was to remain till I came. After proper time for information, went in, defiring Jofeph to let the king know, that I was the man that he expected: upon which he met me with fome complaifance, and feemed to receive me affectionately, inviting me to fit down. Told him that I was the man that wrote two letters to him laft year, one from Monongehela, and the other from Fort Pitt. Afked if he received them with a belt of wampum. He replied that he received all, which he would produce if required. I informed him it was not neceffary, if he received them it was enough. Proceeded to let him know that my defign in coming now, was the fame that was fpecified in the letters—that I was a minifter defirous to inftruct them into the knowledge of that GOD who made us all. That now I was ready to fpeak to him and his peopie, if he would only grant me liberty. Replied that in thefe matters he could do nothing without the advice of his council; that he would inform them of it, and an anfwer fhould be given as foon as the great feaft was ended. This was not only what they call a feaft, but alfo a time

of

of great dancing and gaming, so that nothing else could be attended to till that was finished. To improve the present time, concluded to visit the Moravian towns

SABBATH 14, in company with Mr. Duncan, set out, but by reason of ice, arrived not to it till afternoon. When we came, worship was finishing; the minister continued but a few sentences, which were spoken by him in the English tongue, an interpreter giving the meaning to the Indians. This town is situated on high level land east side of Muskingum, about ten miles up the stream from New-Comer's Town. It is laid out in regular form—houses are built on each side of the street. These Indians moved here about August 1772, and have used such frugality, that they have built neat log houses to dwell in, and a good house for divine worship, about twenty-two feet by eighteen, well seated, and a good floor and chimney. They are a mixture of Stock-Bridge, Mingo, and Delaware Indians. Since the last war their chief residence has been about Wioming. Their conduct in time of worship is praise-worthy. Their grave and solemn countenances exceed what is commonly seen among us at such times. Their minister, the Reverend David Siezberger seems an honest man, a native of Moravia, nor has he been many years in this country. He has been successful among

among thefe poor heathens, condefcending for their fake to endure hardfhips. While I was prefent he ufed no kind of prayer, which was not pleafing to me, therefore afked him if that was their uniform practice. He replied that fome times prayer was ufed. Their worfhip began and ended with finging an hymn in the Indian language, which was performed melodioufly. In the evening they met again for worfhip, but their minifter, inadvertently or by defign, fpoke in the German language, fo that by me nothing was underftood. Mr. Siezberger told me that near eighty families belong to their two towns, and there were two minifters befides himfelf. I was informed that one of them, whofe name is Youngman, is a perfon of good abilities. By what appeared, muft fay, that the conduct of the Moravian fociety towards the heathen is commendable. Thefe have behaved like chriftians indeed, while moft of other focieties have altogether neglected, or in general made but faint attempts.* Indeed by what I have heard of the Reverend David Braynard, he was fincerely engaged, but his time was fhort. In the evening, informed Mr. Siezberger, that it would gratify me to preach to his Indians. He replied with fome appearance of indifference, that an

opportunity

---

* No reference is had to the northern Indians, the author not perfectly knowing their ftate.

opportunity might be had in the morning. 'Tis probable he was a little afraid to countenance me, left fome difciples might be made; than which, nothing was more foreign from my intention. Or his refervednefs may be afcribed to his natural difpofition.

MONDAY 15, parted here with my kind fellow-traveller Mr. Duncan, who went on his way towards Fort Pitt. At the appointed time the Indians convened—Jofeph Peappi was interpreter. Introduced my difcourfe by obferving that it was not my defign in coming from home, to preach to them, not being informed of their removal; but feeing Providence gave an opportunity, had a defire to fpeak to them. Proceeded to obferve that all the difciples of our Saviour JESUS CHRIST feparated themfelves from the courfe of *this* world, no longer to live as the world lived. As other people were bad, they might expect fome difficulties, and perhaps fome perfecutions; but that they fhould be ftrong in heart, for GOD in due time would give them reft. That they fhould be watchful, and beware of backfliding, to live like other Indians; but as GOD had opened their eyes, to keep on their way till they came to eternal reft with CHRIST in heaven, &c. &c. The difcourfe continued about half an hour. On this occafion was very fenfible of divine affiftance; and from the great

and

and apparent folemnity, it was thought that the
word of God was felt with power. Such was
the fpiritual delight enjoyed, that it feemed no
fmall compenfation for my troubles and hardfhips endured. The next town was fituated
about ten miles up the fame ftream, where the
minifters chiefly refide. Was informed that
the other houfe of worfhip was more fplendid,
adorned with a fteeple and bell, but the ice prevented me from feeing it. Thefe Indians are
tradefmen, underftanding farming and carpenter
work; and being already furnifhed with ftock,
intend to live as we do, and 'tis probable in a
few years will live richly; for the land appears
good for wheat. While I was here one of the
Indians afked the minifter, when Eafter Sunday
was? Mr. Siezberger feemed to evade any difcourfe about it, and only told him that it was
not for fome time, and that he fhould have notice before it came. Perhaps had this queftion
been afked among us, I fhould have thought
little about it. But here the cafe was the *reverfe*;
for while I ruminated on it, my foul was filled
with horror to think that *mortal* man fhould
prefume to teach a heathen religioufly to obferve
what God Almighty never taught him as any
part of his will. 'Tis granted, that according
to ecclefiaftical hiftory, this feftival claims antiquity; but the hoary head is a crown of honour
only

only when found in the way of righteoufnefs. And it muft be granted that the holy fcriptures are the only *rule* in matters of religion, by which we are to judge what is right, and what is not. Old errors and fuperftition can never become modern truths. Nor need the difciples of CHRIST give themfelves the leaft trouble to fearch what is called *antiquity* on fuch fubjects; for it fhould be a matter of no more *concern* to them, than to know whether the trees, in Mahomet's *elyfian fields*, are pears or apricots.

MY thoughts were not limited here, but went in fearch of the fuperftitious reliques of the fcarlet whore, yet kept alive among us who call ourfelves REFORMED. And indeed I found many, but am fo well acquainted with the prejudices of education, as to fear that all that might be faid on the fubject, would terminate as it did with *Othaawaapeelethee*, the Shawannee Indian, who faid "they had lived a great while in the way that they now do, and were *refolved* to *continue* fo." Many inftances might be produced, but fhall mention only the obfervance of Chriftmas, which may with more propriety be called POPEMAS. Methinks I fee the reader furprifed at the appelation fo uncommon; but is it not with greater propriety called the *mafs* of him who is the inftitutor of it, than to bear his NAME, who has neither ordained nor will approve of it?

'Tis

'Tis certain that CHRIST never intended any fingular homage to be paid to the day of his birth, which is plain from there being no records of it in the holy fcripture.* This Infinite wifdom thought proper to conceal, as the body of Mofes, to prevent fuperftition. And where fcripture has no mouth to fpeak, we ought to have no ears to hear, nor hearts to obey, for "*his fervants ye are whom ye obey.*" Seeing this is the cafe, will it be uncharitable to call fuch as uphold the reliques of popery, the *worfhippers* of the image of the beaft in thefe particulars? 'Tis common for people to fay, what harm is it to worfhip on this day? May it not be afked fuch, what harm is it to eat meat? but if any fhould tell us it is offered to an *idol,* you know we are not to eat. The cafe is fimilar— 'tis no harm to worfhip, if it is not done as under the notion of C H R I S T M A S; but when that is the motive, 'tis then honouring the whore of Babylon, and confequently no longer a matter of indifferency.—But to proceed, I returned to New-Comer's Town in the afternoon, and went to fee captain Killbuck, who is a fenfible Indian, and ufes us with part of the complaifance of a gentleman. He fpeaks good Englifh, fo that I converfed on the fubject of preaching,

---

* There is no certainty when Chrift was born, whether it was on the firft or twenty-fifth day of December.

preaching, and he was to meet me next morning to converfe further. He invited me to make free in coming to fee him. Soon perceived that he bore the chief fway in all their affairs, and could do more than the king himfelf in many things.

TUESDAY 16, met captain Killbuck, fpoke on many fubjects. In our difcourfe he told me, that fome years fince, two Prefbyterian minifters vifited them—that they did not incline to en-courage their continuance, yet their vifit had fuch effect, that they had been thinking of it ever fince.* He faid, that they intended to have both a minifter and fchoolmafter, but would not have Prefbyterians, because their minifters went to war againft them, and there-fore did not like to be taught by them now, who were before for killing them. It was plain that Indian prejudice was very great and un-reafonable. Replied that the Moravians never fought againft them, therefore they might receive them. His reply was, that Moravians did not belong to our kingdom, being from Germany, and could not fave their people alive in time of war. Upon this he related the diftreffes and dangers of the Moravian Indians laft war, and how they were preferved at Philadelphia. Adding, that for all the affiftance that the

Moravians

* Minifters do good when they know it not.

Moravians could give, their Indians might have been killed. Hence argued, that it did not fignify to be of that religion, that could not protect them in war time. He faid, they intended to go to England and fee our king, and tell him that they would be of the fame religion that he is, and would defire a minifter and fchoolmafter of his own choofing. Told him that his fpeech pleafed me, but thought they were too poor to accomplifh it, and feared they would get little affiftance. He faid, that they had near forty pounds already, and intended to make an early hunt, which would enable them to go in the fall. To effect this, captain Killbuck and Swallowhead were chofen meffengers to *Sir William Johnfon* while I was there. Encouraged their defigns, willing to refign the civilizing them to his majefty's directions : but am perfuaded, that the fervice of the church of England, as it now ftands, will never be prefcribed for Indians; for nothing would difguft them more than to have a religion, which would confume the greater part of life, only to learn its ceremonies.

THURSDAY 18, Afternoon, converfing with Killbuck, he told me that the young men were defirous to hear me preach, confequently concluded to preach next day. In the evening, had an opportunity to converfe with Jofeph Peappi, who

who would interpret for me; but I told him
that I would give only five pounds for a month;
he faid, he ufed to have feven pounds. Indians,
from the greateft to the leaft, feem mercenary
and exceffively greedy of gain. Indeed they
are fo lazy, that they are commonly needy, and
muft be more fo, if they do not cultivate their
lands; deer grow fo fcarce, that, great part of the
year, many of them rather ftarve than live. Mr.
Evans, who is a trader in this town, told me,
that laft fummer fome were fupported by fuck-
ing the juice of green cornftalks.

FRIDAY 19, expected to preach, but Killbuck
told me that they were not yet fully united in
the point—Had reafon to think that the king
was not much for it, though he faid little—Neither do I conclude that Jofeph was very defirous
of it, for the traders often told me that the
Moravians taught their Indians to difrefpect
other focieties, and I could wifh that there were
lefs grounds for the report. Afked Killbuck if
he knew the reafon why they were not united
for my preaching? he feemed to intimate, it
would have been otherwife, if I had come laft
fall, while they were in the notion of it: but
found, by converfing with him, there is a jeal-
oufy in them, left we fhould have fome defign
of enflaving them, or fomething of that nature.
He told me that an highland officer took one of
their

their women as his wife, and went with her into
Maryland about Joppa: and they heard, there
he fold her a flave like a negro. This he faid,
a gentleman in Philadelphia told him: and as
they never faw the fquaa afterwards, they were
ready to believe that the report was true. If
this cafe is fo, and this gentleman could only fee
that by his means he has prejudiced the heathens
againft us, am perfuaded he would mentally
retract his intelligence with a degree of forrow.
Replied, that I never heard it before, yet was
perfuaded that it could not be true, that fhe continued a flave; for if the officer was guilty of
fuch a crime, the law of our land allowed no
Indians of our country to be flaves, and the
magiftrates would furely fet her free. But he
faid, their people did not know our law, therefore fuch reports made them afraid of us. He
further faid, " What is become of the woman,
fhe never came back to us again?" Replied,
that I could not tell, may be fhe did not choofe
to come, or fhe might be dead. By this time,
was much difcouraged, and by hardfhips and
want of provifions my health and ftrength were
greatly impaired. No meat could be had here
for love or money. Bought milk at nine-pence
a quart, and butter at two fhillings a pound, but
not near fufficient could be had. From the
king, had bought the rump of a deer dried, after

their

their cuftom, in the fmoke to preferve it without falt, which made it fo difagreeable that little could be ufed. Indeed, I had coffee, chocolate and tea, but fugar was fo fcarce, that it could not well be ufed. Defires called for a land, where famine doth not raife her baleful head, therefore on Saturday 20, inquired for a pilate to accompany me towards Ohio. The feafon was feverely cold, fo that the king and captain Killbuck would not fuffer me to go, for they faid the weather was fo cold, that it would kill even an Indian. Indeed the feafon was fo intenfely cold, that attempts to travel were impracticable. My continuance here was very difagreeable; for though the traders of this town were civil, yet they had no tafte for religion, fo that I was alone without fuitable fuftenance, waiting the permiffion of Providence to depart homewards.

SABBATH 21, this was a remarkable cold day—fome part of it was fpent converfing with Killbuck on feveral particulars, concerning the belief of the Delaware Indians. 'Twas afked, whether they believed that there is a GOD who created all things ? He replied, that this was their common belief. The fecond queftion was, whether they believed that when any perfon died, their foul went to a happy ftate, or to a ftate of mifery ? Replied, this they alfo believed.

The

The third was, whether they knew that God would by his great power raife up all the dead to life again at the end of this world? His reply was, that this they knew nothing of, 'till lately they had heard it among the Moravian Indians. Thefe Indians have been fo long acquainted with us, that it is not eafy to determine what they have learned of us.

THIS day liberty was granted to preach as often as I pleafed, but not having my interpreter, could do little; for Killbuck would not accept of Jofeph, for, he faid, I might as well not fpeak as to have him, for inftead of faying what I faid, Jofeph would fay what his own heart thought. Though I had better thoughts of Jofeph, foon perceived that Killbuck had fuch an averfion to him, that if he was ufed for an interpreter, nothing could be done. This was the only time that opened for doing good, and this opportunity was chiefly loft, for want of Mr. Owens my old interpreter; therefore all that was faid as preaching, was in the council, ufing Killbuck as an interpreter, who was capable in common affairs, but knew little concerning religion. To day the king and council concluded, that no more rum fhould be drank in this town or nation, and that there fhould be no more gaming or dancing only at their triennial feaft. This made me think of the laws of New-Jerfey about *horferacing*,

horferacing, in which there were fuch referves, as evidently demonftrated that fome of the affembly loved the *fport*.

MONDAY 22, Killbuck told me that they were making up a fpeech to governor Penn who had wrote to them laft fall, and I muft wait to write and carry it. He faid they would provide me a pilate.

TUESDAY 23, the fame meffage was fent, informing me that for fix dollars, fhould have a pilate to fee me over Ohio. This news was not the moft agreeable, as the wages were unreafonable, and my daily experices fimilar. 'Twas impoffible to purchafe one pound of bear's flefh, or one venifon ham.—This people live truly poor. The land is indeed good, but at prefent the price is in the hand of fools. In the afternoon a meffenger came for me to wait on the king and council—Their number might be about twenty convened in their council-houfe, which may be fixty feet by twenty-four. It had one poft in the middle, and two fires. Moft of them had long pipes in almoft conftant ufe— they fet round the fires on fkins—a ftool was prepared for me—then prefented a bowl of hommany, of which they were eating. Spoons they had none, but a fmall ladle ferves four or five Indians. After our repaft, a fheet of paper was brought, and Killbuck being interpreter, informed

formed me, that it was their defire that I fhould write to governor Penn from them, defiring that he would inform his people, that if any brought rum their fide of Allegini river or Ohio, they had appointed fix men, on pain of death, to ftave every keg—And that he would let governor Franklin know, that they defired all the Jerfey Indians to move into their country, as it is large enough, &c. Accordingly a letter was written, and every word interpreted by captain Killbuck and an affiftant. This was delivered to his honour Richard Penn, efq. 'Tis to be hoped the contents thereof will merit his honour's attention; for as the Indians feemed refolute in the point, 'tis poffible that neglects might be attended with undefirable confequences.

WEDNESDAY 24, was called to the council, and defired to deliver a fpeech to the Quakers at Philadelphia; but as there was nothing worthy of writing in the meffage, therefore delivered it verbally to Mr. Thomas Wharton in Philadelphia.

As next day I was to begin my journey towards Ohio, therefore it may be faid, that at this meeting, I took my leave of them, giving them all the advice that was thought expedient, which they feemed to receive very friendly—fo we parted in love and peace.

THESE

THESE Indians are not defective in natural abilities, and their long acquaintance with us, has given fome of them better notions than many other favages. They are as void of civil government as the Shawannees. Their virtues are but few, their vices near the fame with other Indians. Their cuftoms are refembling the Shawannees, only they have a great feaft once in three years. Afked Killbuck the meaning of it? he faid, it might have had fome meaning at firft, but now was obferved only as an old cuftom. The language of thefe Indians in general differs very much from the Shawannees, being ftill more guttural. Shall give you a fpecimen of their manner of counting to ten, viz *guitta, nufha, nucha, neah, pelenah, cootafh neefhafh, chaafh, pefhcung, telen.* Thefe Indians at prefent have no way of worfhipping or acknowledging GOD; but they feem to incline to learn to read —and have begun to farm, to which they are much affifted by a Jerfey Indian, who is not only their fmith, but alfo makes their ploughs. Indeed it appears that both a minifter and fchoolmafter may go among them with fafety and fuccefs, if they keep their conclufion to fuffer no rum to be brought into their country. On this fubject I fpoke much, fhewing the advantages that would arife from the conftant obfervance of this conclufion; and exhorted

them

them to be *ftrong*.* To which they anfwered
with loud voices *kehellah*, which is the moft
emphatical way of faying yes. They fhew fome
honour to a minifter; but are fo extortionate in
the price of their provifions, that a man muft
expend much more money in preaching among
them, than he can get by preaching among us.
They increafe much fafter than the Shawannees,
poligamy not being fo common. Their town
is in no regular form. Neither thefe nor the
Shawannees claim any diftinct property in lands,
looking on it that GOD made it free for all.
Nor could I underftand that they have any
fixed bounds to a nation, efteeming it chiefly
ufeful for hunting. Providence feems to point
out the civilizing of thefe Indians; for a farming life will lead to laws, learning, and government, to fecure property. Captain Killbuck
told me, he faw the neceffity of a magiftrate to
recover debts, and faid, that by and by, he expected that they would have one; but as yet
their people did not underftand matters. 'Tis a
little furprifing that *Proteftants* fhould be fo
neglectful of the Indians; and in common there
is no concern appears among them, about civilizing the many nations, that are yet rude
favages: while on the other hand, the *French*
Papifts

* This is an Indian phrafe, fignifying as much as to fay, be
refolute, firm and valiant.

Papifts have been very induftrious to inftil their principles into the minds of fuch as were contiguous to them, and with fome fuccefs. The Waindots are a little tainted, but might, 'tis probable, be eafily better informed, and efpecially as the French are in a manner expelled. This I can fay, that though my body and eftate fuffered by this journey, yet I do not repent my vifit, but rejoice that fome attempts have been made, though not with the fuccefs that could be wifhed. Would have ftayed longer, but being deftitute of my old interpreter, and fcarcity of provifions, rendered it impracticable.

THURSDAY 25, having a pilate, which coft fix dollars, though I paid Mr. Tompfon the trader only one guinea, yet he made it up in goods, fet out about eleven o'clock from New-Comer's Town on Mufkingum, intending the neareft courfe for the river Ohio. My pilate was a Jerfey Indian, whofe name is Pontus Newtemus; he fpoke Englifh intelligibly, but was almoft as great a ftranger to the woods as myfelf—and we had a path only the firft part of the way. Our courfe fhould be a little fouth of eaft. This day travelled only about fifteen miles, and encamped by a brook, where we were furrounded with abundance of howling wolves. Spent the evening converfing on many

fubjects;

fubjects; found Pontus with little more knowledge than other Indians.—Affifted by a good
fire, we flept well, confidering that our frigid
curtains were the circumambient air.

FRIDAY 26, fet out about eight o'clock. This
day we left our little path, and went according
to my directions, for Pontus knew not the
courfe, only he was informed from a rough
fketch of the new map which I had by me.
Some part of the way the land was charming—
looked extraordinary for wheat, covered with
the fineft blackoak trees and goofberry-bufhes;
at laft encamped at a creek about five yards
wide, running foutheaft, neither of us knew into
what larger creek it emptied. Surrounded with
the protection of him, whofe tender mercies are
over the works of his hands, we flept fafe in the
midft of a doleful wildernefs.—This day's journey was at leaft thirty miles.

SATURDAY 27, fet out, and foon left the creek,
fteered our courfe near eaft, till at laft we came
to a creek which we followed, and a little before funfet, came to the river Ohio, oppofite to
Weeling. This creek empties into Ohio oppofite to an ifland, and as it is common to pafs
down Ohio the eaft fide of this ifland, by that
means it efcaped the notice of Mr. Hutchins,
and alfo of Mr. Hooper, confequently it was
not in my map, therefore could not tell where

I

I was. Mr. Hooper has now rectified this defect, and was pleased to give the creek my name.

SABBATH 28, in the morning, parted with my pilate in great love and friendship, having travelled at leaſt ſeventy-five miles together in the ſolitary wilderneſs; and though he always behaved well, can't ſay that I was without ſome fear at times, leſt he ſhould do me an injury. Went four or five miles down Ohio, and came oppoſite to Mr. William Mᶜ Mechens, from whence I took water for the Shawannees. Much ice was driving down the ſtream, yet when I called, Mr. Mᶜ Mechen ventured over in a little canoe, that threatened danger, leaving at that time my horſe behind, we came ſafely over. When we arrived to this ſhore, my ſenſation was truly pleaſing, hope raiſed high expectations of ſeeing New-Jerſey once more. Here remained for ſome weeks, waiting for the arrival of my brother and Mr. Clark, who were gone for corn to Monongehela. And as I am now about leaving this famous country, think proper to ſpeak a little on a ſubject chiefly omitted.

THE land, according to my judgment, has been juſtly deſcribed; but this is not all the excellency of this new world, for its waters abound with the greateſt abundance of fine fiſhes.

fifhes. There is a kind of fifh here called white
perch, fome of which are larger than a fhad, and
very agreeable food. Sun-fifh, or what is called
yellow-perch, are here as large as a fhad. There
is another kind of fifh called buffaloe fifh, many
of which are larger than our fheepfhead—Catfifh of an extraordinary fort are taken here, fome
of which are faid to weigh an hundred pounds.
We took one, that after feven of us had eaten
twice of it, part was given to the Indians.
Large falmon are to be met with here alfo—
fome fturgeon, prodigious large pike, chubs,
mullets, and various kinds of fmall fifhes. I
have been informed that fhad have been taken,
and fome herrings; but the riches of the waters
are not fully known, the people not having
feines made as yet. The wild beafts met with
here, are bears, wolves, panthers, wildcats, foxes,
raccoons, beavers, otters, and fome few fquirrils
and rabbits; buffaloes, deer and elks, called by
the Delawares *moos*. The fowls to be feen are
wildgeefe, ducks of various kinds, fome fwans,
abundance of turkies, fome of which are very
large; pheafants, pigeons, and fome few quails
by fome called partridges. This country promifes the inhabitants a plentitude of the neceffaries of life; and having defcribed it according
to my knowledge, and beft information, would
have here left the reader: but as God was
pleafed

pleafed to bring me through fome very trying fcenes, thought proper to communicate the fame, hoping it may be of fome benefit to fuch as meet with tribulations, in this world of forrow.

FRIDAY, March 19, left Ohio alone, and encamped on the creek called Weeling. This was the only night that I flept alone in the wildernefs : the folitary repofe can fcarcely be defcribed, many thoughts arofe, none otherwife to be removed, only by the proper exercife of faith on him, who has promifed never to leave nor forfake his children. It was fo ordered that not even a wolf howled to difturb me.

MARCH 25, was croffing the Alegini mountain—the fnow was nine inches deep, and fuffered not a little by the fevere cold.

SABBATH 28, came to Old Town, and preached in the evening at Col. Craffop's. On the week following, was taken with the pleurify, and lay at David Bowen's, at Conegocheage.

SATURDAY, April 3, drew off about fourteen ounces of blood, which relieved fo much, that in the afternoon, fell into a pleafant fleep, and had fuch a reprefentation of my family at home, that after awaking, told fome of the people, that it was my belief that my fon was dead, and found when I came home, he had departed
about

about that hour. From that time my fpirit funk in me, with an unaccountable fadnefs. From this infer, that God doth fometimes give intimations of future events in fleep.* But in common, no notice fhould be taken of flumbering imaginations. After recruiting my ftrength a little, went through New-Caftle county, having fome bufinefs to tranfact there.

THURSDAY, April 22, fet out in hopes of feeing my family once more in the land of the living, but about fixteen miles from Philadelphia, at a fmall town called Chefter, met an acquaintance, who gave me the forrowful news that my favourite *fon* was dead. Though this news was expected, yet when it verbally reached my ears, it ftruck me through the very heart, with fuch extacies of forrow, that my foul feemed as if it would expire. Sorrowfully I rode to Philadelphia, and was prevailed on to remain there over the Sabbath. Had buried two children before, but as Jacob's heart and life was bound up in Benjamin, fo was mine in this fon. At this time, life feemed a burden, and all the world a mere empty nothing. Sleep was only obtained when exhaufted with weeping.

SATURDAY 24, in the morning when I awoke, the wounds began to bleed afrefh: but, unexpectedly,

* Job xxxiii. 15.

15

pectedly, thefe words came with fuch power, that relief was foon obtained, *viz.* "My fon "defpife not the chaftening of the Lord, nor "faint when thou art rebuked of him: for whom "the Lord loveth, he chafteneth, and fcourgeth "every fon whom he receiveth." That part of the verfe in particular, which fays, "whom the "Lord loveth, he fcourgeth," was of fingular fupport in my prefent diftrefs; impreffing on my heart fuch a fenfe of God's love to me, that fuch was the relief, that the next day, was ena-bled to preach. The words are in Heb. xii. 5, 6. what a precious faying is that! which fo comfortably affirms, " that whatfoever things "were written aforetime, were written for our "learning; that we through patience and com-"FORT of the fcriptures might have hope." There is no condition, in which any of God's children can be, but he hath left a word fuited exactly to their cafe. And indeed it muft be fo, feeing that his promife is " I will never leave "thee nor forfake thee."

MONDAY 26, fet out, and at night lodged at a friend's houfe. When retired to my bed-chamber, thoughts crowded into my foul—The forrowful fcene began to open to view, antici-pating my arrival to meet my beloved wife, in my abfence, bereaved of a dear fon. Ideas of my darling came frefh into my foul—I knew
not

not how to go home and mifs him. Circum-
ftances of his death came into mind, how hard
it was to leave him alive, and find him dead!
what is common to human nature in diftrefs,
fruitlefs wifhes were not a few: fuch as, oh!
that I had been with him, or even had been
permitted to attend his *dear remains* to the
folitary grave! but now, alas! alas! I fhall
never more fee him on earth!—Thefe thoughts
with many of the fame nature, were productive
of floods of tears 'till fleep gave refpite.

TUESDAY 27, in the morning, foon after I
awoke, while ruminating on my cafe, thefe
words were impreffed on my heart with both
power and comfort, viz. " ye have heard of the
" afflictions of Job, and have feen the end of the
" Lord; that the Lord is very pitiful, and of
" tender mercy." The whole dealings of God
towards Job opened very clearly to view, and it
was evident that his cafe far exceeded mine: at
once he loft all his children and wealth, not by
what we call a natural Death, but by one fatal
ftroke the vital flame is quenched in the ruins
of an houfe. That claufe which faith, " the
Lord is very pitiful," miniftered truly great comfort to my foul. Had then a lively fenfe of the
tender compaffion of the Lord; and though he
caufeth grief for wife ends, yet will he have
compaffion according to the multitude of his
mercies.

mercies. By this means, found myself much supported, and enabled to believe that I should yet find God very pitiful, notwithstanding that now the chastisement was severe. The words are in the epistle of James, chap. v. and verse 11, only with this variation, viz. in James the word is *patience*, and the word *affliction* was used instead thereof, as being most suitable to my case. It may be observed, that in giving comfort, the Lord doth not always use the very word in the text, but is pleased to adapt the *substance* thereof, according to the circumstance of the afflicted. 'Tis more than probable, that there are some, who are strangers to comfort from the scriptures by the application of promises, and such may think it only a kind of fancy; but they who are better acquainted with God, and know the mysteries of the kingdom, can bless his holy name, for such glorious displays of his love.

As I came within a few miles of home, sorrow returned again afresh in such a degree, that human nature seemed too weak to sustain the heavy *load*, till these words were impressed on my mind with a degree of power, viz. "Can a woman forget her sucking child, that she should not have compassion on the son of her womb? Yea, they may forget, yet will I not forget thee." For a little space, that part calmed the surges of
sorrow,

forrow, which fays, " yet will I not forget thee."
But had not rode far before my wounds began
to bleed afrefh; then thefe words came with fuch
power, that not only my diftrefs was removed,
but alfo greater affurance of eternal life was
enjoyed, than what I had been favoured with
for fome years paft, viz. " that we muft through
much tribulation enter into the kingdom of
GOD." Being thus fupported, came home in
the ftrength of the LORD, having great caufe to
fpeak both of judgment and mercy. This tour
contained fix months and one day, in which
greater hardfhips were endured, than are fpoken
of, but may be conceived by remembring that
in rainy and fnowy weather blankets ftretched
were all my houfe: and in fair weather no other
fhelter than the open air: but in many refpects,
have learned more in this time, than in all my
life before. In the defcription of this country,
and account of the Indians, my endeavour and
view was, to inform all who were pleafed to
read: but the narrative, refpecting my troubles,
was chiefly defigned for the fons and daughters
of affliction, hoping it may not be altogether in
vain to others. To all parents of children, who
may be pleafed to read, would clofe this Journal
with a few words of advice. viz.

1. CONSIDER the moft lovely child only lent
to you from GOD, who has a fovereign right to
call

call for his own, when, and in what way feem-
eth good unto himfelf; and none fhould fay,
what doeft thou? Alas! we are prone to forget this, and act as if there was none that ruleth
above, ordering all events here on earth.

2. NEVER fuffer your affections to be fixed
too much on any child, for our children are all
mortal, and at beft but uncertain comforts.
How often may it be obferved, that GOD is
pleafed to take away the flower of a family?
and that in the morning of days and bloom of
life. He has wife ends in all his proceedings,
and gives no account of his actions to man. If
he is pleafed to fpare our children, how often
doth it prove only a continued caufe of forrow?
for fuch is the corruption of the age, that very
few feek after GOD, and endeavour to keep
themfelves unfpotted from the world. We are
too fubject, if GOD endows our children with
any thing diftinguifhable, to idolize fuch; but
often he fhews us our fault, with broken hearts.
This was my unhappy cafe. All my concern
was about my fon Jofeph. He was as dear to
me as Abfalom to David, or as Benjamin to
Jacob. But, was foon made to fee my folly,
and the great inftability of worldly comforts.
All that I would fay on this occafion is, "the
LORD giveth, and the LORD taketh away, bleffed
be the name of the LORD." We find that GOD
makes

makes his dearest children pass under the rod:
and this we may expect, though we are not at
ease; for our blessed Lord says, " as many as I
love, I rebuke and chasten."

3. ENDEAVOUR to be single-hearted, not loving
the world, nor the things of the world, for,
when this is our case, we are fit to live or die;
having our affections on things above, far from
all disappointment. 'Tis said this is not our rest,
and so we shall find it; but there remains a rest
for the people of GOD. 'Tis but a little while,
before all our concerns about this world will
have an end.———Some of our children have
gone before us, and we shall soon follow after;
these bodies shall remain in the solitary confines
of the grave 'till time shall be no more. How
are we disquieted in vain! for all things here
are but vanity and vexation of spirit.

4. AND lastly, when in adversity, beware of
murmuring against GOD. Cannot say that I was
free from it, but am so far from justifying it, that
'tis expected, that among other iniquities, this
also is washed away by the precious blood of
CHRIST. We find this sin cleaving to the best
of men. Jeremiah curses the day of his birth.
'Tis indeed a great evil—it represents GOD lacking wisdom or goodness in disposing events on
earth: but he is wise in all his providences, and
not only good, but he doeth good continually,

and

and nothing but what is for the beſt to all his children. David could ſay, it was good for him to have been afflicted. And we have this gracious word to ſupport us, viz. " all things do work together for good to them that love GOD." Wherefore let us lift up our hands that hang down, and be encouraged, for whatſoever we ſuffer, it is the LORD that has done it, and can direct it, and bleſs it for good. He is at hand himſelf, and while we are here, let him be the delight and joy of our hearts, then we may ſay with calmneſs, when our ſpirits are demanded, come LORD JESUS, come quickly, amen.

F I N I S.

*To complete the sheet, it is hoped, these Hymns
may be acceptable, as their substance is truly
evangelical; they became favourites of the
Editor by hearing them frequently used on
the banks of the Ohio.*

The SINNER'S *Invitation, &c.*

COME, sinners attend,
 And make no delay,
Good news from a friend
 I bring you to day:
Glad news of salvation,
 Come now and receive,
There's no condemnation
 To you that believe.

I AM that I AM
 Hath sent me to you,
Glad news to proclaim,
 Your foes to subdue:
To you, O distressed,
 Afflicted, forlorn,
Whose sins are increased,
 And cannot be borne.

But

But ſtill if you cry,
    O what is his name?
This is his reply,
    I AM that I AM:
His name (though myſterious)
    Will fully ſupply
Their wants, howe'er various
    That unto him fly.

Exhauſtleſs and full
    For-ever his ſtore;
Then look no more dull
    Tho' never ſo poor.
Tho' blind, lame and feeble,
    And helpleſs you lie,
He's willing and able,
    Your wants to ſupply.

Then only believe,
    And truſt in his name,
He will not deceive,
    Nor put you to ſhame:
But fully ſupply you
    With all things in ſtore,
Nor will he deny you
    Becauſe you are poor:

The convinced Sinner coming to CHRIST.

THE SECOND PART.

DEAR JESUS, here comes,
    And knocks at thy door,
A beggar for crumbs,
    Diftreffed and poor:
Blind, lame and forfaken,
    All roll'd in his blood,
At laft overtaken,
    When running from GOD.

To afk childrens bread
    I dare not prefume,
But, LORD, to be fed
    With fragments I come:
Some crumbs from thy table,
    O let me obtain,
For lo, Thou art able
    My wants to fuftain.

I own I deferve
    No favour to fee,
So long I did fwerve,
    And wander from Thee;

'Till

'Till brought by affliction
    My follies to mourn;
Now under conviction
    To Thee I return.

Great God, my defert
    Is nothing but death,
And hence to depart
    For-ever in wrath;
Yet, Lord, to this city
    Of refuge I flee,
O let thine eye pity
    A finner like me!

For fince Thou haft faid,
    Thou wilt caft out none
That flee to thine aid,
    As finners undone:
Now, Lord, I am come as
    Condemned to die,
And on this fweet promife
    I humbly rely.

I cannot depart,
    Dear Jesus, nor yield
'Till feels my poor heart
    This promife fulfill'd,
That I may for-ever
    A monument be
To praife the free Saviour
    Of finners like me.

The great affize.

L O, th' Almighty King of glory,
  Sends his awful fummons forth!
Calls the nations all before him
    From the eaft, fouth, weft and north!
His loud trumpet, his loud trumpet, his loud
      trumpet
    Rends the tombs, the dead awake!

Now behold the dead arifing;
  Great and fmall before him ftand:
Not one foul forgot, or miffing;
  None his orders countermand.
All ftand waiting, all ftand waiting, all ftand
      waiting
    For their laft decifive doom.

Now the SAVIOUR, once defpifed,
  Comes to judge the quick and dead;
See his foes, each one with horror,
  Lifting up his guilty head.
How they tremble! how they tremble! how they
      tremble
    At the LAMB's tremendous bar!

                                    Now

Now they fee him on the rainbow,
    With his countlefs guards around :
Saints and angels his retinue,
    With their harps of fweeteft found,
Hallelujah ! hallelujah ! hallelujah !
    Echoes fweet from all the choir.

Now his chofen gladly meet him,
    All feraphic, all divine !
Lo, they join the glorious army
    Whofe bright robes the fun outfhine !
All triumphant ! all triumphant ! all triumph-
        ant !
    See the grand redeemed throng !

Then behold the dreadful fentence
    On the foes of CHRIST is paft :
Down to hell without repentance
    All the guilty crowd is caft,
While the ranfom'd, while the ranfom'd, while
        the ranfom'd,
    All applaud the righteous doom.

Now attend the noble army,
    Wafh'd in their REDEEMER's blood ;
Swift and joyful is their journey,
    To the palace of their GOD !
All victorious ! all victorious ! all victorious !
    Hallelujah to the L A M B !

Epiphonema.

O ye Sinners, now give glory
    To the great eternal Three!
While such danger lies before you,
    Can you unconcerned be?
Judgment haſtens! judgment haſtens! judgment
    hastens!
    Mercy, mercy now implore!

Printed in The Republic of China